SOCIAL MISSION STATEMENT

INTRODUCTION
Celtic Football Club is legendary and as with most legends as much myth as fact surrounds its history and what the Club stands for today. The Social Mission Statement aims to simply define what the Club stands for and seeks to promote within society.

HISTORY
Celtic Football Club was founded in 1888. Its principal founder was a Marist Brother named Walfrid. The Club had two principal aims: The first aim was to raise funds to provide food for the poor of the East End of Glasgow, an area of the City that was greatly impoverished and had a high rate of infant mortality. Within the East End was a large Irish community and friction was growing between the native Glaswegians and the new influx of Irish. Brother Walfrid saw the need for social integration and his vision was for a football club that Scottish and Irish, Protestants and Catholics alike could support. A new football club would be a vehicle to bring the communities together and this was the second aim. The Marist brother sought for the Club to have both a Scottish and Irish identity and hence, the Club's name "Celtic" came about, representing a bridge of cultures across the Irish Sea.

CURRENT POSITIONING OF CELTIC FOOTBALL CLUB
Celtic Football Club is a Scottish football club with proud Irish links. The primary business of Celtic is as a football club. It is run on a professional business basis with no political agenda. However, the Club has a wider role and the responsibility of being a major Scottish social institution promoting health, well-being and social integration.

WHO IS CELTIC FOOTBALL CLUB FOR?
Celtic Football Club is for people who want to support a football club that strives for excellence in Scotland and in Europe, is proud of its history, supportive of its local community and seeks to support the following aims: "To maximise all opportunities to disassociate the Club from sectarianism and bigotry of any kind. To promote Celtic as a Club for all people, regardless of gender, age, religion, race or ability."

SUMMARY
Celtic is a club for everyone who believes in football as a medium for healthy pleasure, entertainment and social integration. The Club always has been and always will simply aim to be the team of the people.

Photographs supplied by Scottish News and Sport (SNS).

Statistics compiled by Paul Cuddihy, Joe Sullivan,
Mark Henderson, Laura Brannan and Frank Hannaway.
All information/statistics correct as of June 19, 2012.

Production by Michael McGuinness, design by Colin Sumpter,
Sport Media.

Printed in Slovenia by arrangement with KINT Ljubljana.

CONTENTS

THE SUPPORT PLAYED THEIR PART IN TITLE WIN

THIS time last year I said that I was delighted to see the return of the Wee Green Book and I'm even more delighted this year to be writing these words as the manager of the SPL champions for season 2011/12.

From the outset, that was our No.1 target and nothing has changed – it is our aim to ensure that the trophy and the championship flag remain at Celtic Park, and it is also our goal to improve on last season.

We were unlucky last term not to increase our silverware haul as both the League Cup, after reaching the final, and the Scottish Cup, where we went out at the semi-final stage, were within our grasp and with a little bit of luck we could have done better in both competitions. Still, that has only made us more determined to deliver more success this season.

Of course, lifting the title last season opened the door to the opportunity of UEFA Champions League football once more and, again, that is an area where we want to gain a further foothold as we all know how much the European nights mean to Celtic supporters.

And, talking of our fans, I have to say that the backing last season was tremendous and I know just how much the players took from that support throughout the season.

I've been in the crowd as a Celtic fan, I've felt the hairs on the back of my neck stand up as a Celtic player and I've also been lucky enough to experience the thunder as Celtic manager, so I know exactly how big a part the supporters played in last season's title triumph. So it goes without saying that the same backing this season will go a long way to helping achieve further success.

I know I said I wanted the thunder back at Celtic Park, but it is the support that have delivered that thunder so they can take the credit for the atmosphere that now lights up our games both home and away. I hope you can all join us once more this coming season on what will hopefully be another journey towards another championship.

Neil Lennon
Manager
Celtic Football Club

celticfactfile

CLUB HONOURS

SCOTTISH LEAGUE WINNERS (43 Times)
1892/93, 1893/94, 1895/96, 1897/98, 1904/05, 1905/06, 1906/07, 1907/08, 1908/09, 1909/10, 1913/14, 1914/15, 1915/16, 1916/17, 1918/19, 1921/22, 1925/26, 1935/36, 1937/38, 1953/54, 1965/66, 1966/67, 1967/68, 1968/69, 1969/70, 1970/71, 1971/72, 1972/73, 1973/74, 1976/77, 1978/79, 1980/81, 1981/82, 1985/86, 1987/88, 1997/98, 2000/01, 2001/02, 2003/04, 2005/06, 2006/07, 2007/08, 2011/12

SCOTTISH CUP WINNERS (35 Times)
1892, 1899, 1900, 1904, 1907, 1908, 1911, 1912, 1914, 1923, 1925, 1927, 1931, 1933, 1937, 1951, 1954, 1965, 1967, 1969, 1971, 1972, 1974, 1975, 1977, 1980, 1985, 1988, 1989, 1995, 2001, 2004, 2005, 2007, 2011

LEAGUE CUP WINNERS (14 Times)
1956/57, 1957/58, 1965/66, 1966/67, 1967/68, 1968/69, 1969/70, 1974/75, 1982/83, 1997/98, 1999/00, 2000/01, 2005/06, 2008/09

EUROPEAN CUP WINNERS 1967

CORONATION CUP WINNERS 1953

CELTIC PLC DIRECTORS

CELTIC PLC DIRECTORS
Ian Bankier
Peter Lawwell
Eric Riley
Dermot Desmond
Tom Allison
Brian Duffy
Brian Wilson
Ian Livingston
CFAC DIRECTORS
Peter Lawwell
Eric Riley
John Keane
Michael McDonald
Kevin Sweeney
MANAGER
Neil Lennon
ASSISTANT MANAGER
Johan Mjallby

FIRST-TEAM COACH
Garry Parker
HEAD OF YOUTH
Chris McCart
FOOTBALL DEVELOPMENT MANAGER
John Park
KIT CONTROLLER
John Clark
CLUB DOCTOR AND HEAD OF SPORT AND EXERCISE MEDICINE
Roddy Macdonald
HEAD PHYSIOTHERAPIST
Tim Williamson
HEAD OF EXERCISE SCIENCE
Kenny McMillan

CLUB DIRECTORY & RECORDS

CELTIC FOOTBALL CLUB
Celtic Park, Glasgow, G40 3RE

CELTIC CALL CENTRE
Tel: 0871 226 1888
(calls cost up to 10p per minute, telecoms provider dependent. Mobile and other provider charges may vary)

WEBSITE: www.celticfc.net
FORMED: 1888
STADIUM: Celtic Park
CAPACITY: 60,506

HOME STRIP COLOUR
Green/white hooped shirts, white shorts, white socks

AWAY STRIP COLOUR
Black

RECORD ATTENDANCE
92,000 v Rangers, 1938

RECORD VICTORY
11-0 v Dundee, 1895

RECORD DEFEAT
0-8 v Motherwell, 1937

MOST LEAGUE GOALS IN ONE SEASON
50 – Jimmy McGrory, 1935/36

MOST PREMIER/SPL GOALS IN ONE SEASON
35 – Brian McClair, 1986/87
35 – Henrik Larsson, 2000/01

43 NUMBER OF TIMES CELTIC HAS WON THE SCOTTISH LEAGUE CHAMPIONSHIP

THE CELTIC FOOTBALL CLUB
1888

1888-2013

DON'T MISS A GAME!

MATCHDAY TICKETS AVAILABLE FROM THE FOLLOWING OUTLETS:

CALL : 0871 226 1888*

VISIT : CELTICFC.NET

SHOP : TICKET OFFICE

THIS SEASON, WE'RE CELEBRATING OUR 125TH ANNIVERSARY, AND THIS HISTORIC OCCASION WOULDN'T BE THE SAME WITHOUT YOU. SO JOIN US FOR EVERY MATCH - 125 YEARS OF CELTIC!

2012/13
SEASON

CELTIC FC FIXTURES 2012/13

DATE	DAY	OPPONENT	COMPETITION	SCORE
31 Jul/1 Aug	Tue/Wed		CL, Q3 L1	
4 Aug	**Sat**	**Aberdeen**	**SPL 1**	
07/08 Aug	Tue/Wed		CL Q3, L2	
18 Aug	Sat	Ross County	SPL 3	
21/22 Aug	Tue/Wed		CL Play-off, L1	
25 Aug	Sat	Inverness CT	SPL 4	
28/29 Aug	Tue/Wed		CL Play-off, L2	
1 Sep	**Sat**	**Hibernian**	**SPL 5**	
15 Sep	Sat	St Johnstone	SPL 6	
18/19 Sep	Tue/Wed		CL MD1	
22 Sep	**Sat**	**Club 12**	**SPL 7**	
25/26 Sep	Tue/Wed		League Cup R3	
29 Sep	Sat	Motherwell	SPL 8	
02/03 Oct	Tue/Wed		CL MD2	
06 Oct	**Sat**	**Hearts**	**SPL 9**	
20 Oct	Sat	St Mirren	SPL 10	
23/24 Oct	Tue/Wed		CL MD3	
27 Oct	**Sat**	**Kilmarnock**	**SPL 11**	
30/31 Oct	Tue/Wed		League Cup Q/F	
3 Nov	Sat	Dundee United	SPL 12	
6/7 Nov	Tue/Wed		CL MD4	
10 Nov	**Sat**	**St Johnstone**	**SPL 13**	
17 Nov	Sat	Aberdeen	SPL 14	
20/21 Nov	Tue/Wed		CL MD5	
24 Nov	**Sat**	**Inverness CT**	**SPL 15**	
28 Nov	Wed	Hearts	SPL 16	
1 Dec	Sat		Scottish Cup R4	
4/5 Dec	Tue/Wed		CL MD6	
8 Dec	Sat	Kilmarnock	SPL 17	
15 Dec	**Sat**	**St Mirren**	**SPL 18**	
22 Dec	**Sat**	**Ross County**	**SPL 19**	
26 Dec	Wed	Club 12	SPL 20	
29 Dec	Sat	Hibernian	SPL 21	
2 Jan	**Wed**	**Motherwell**	**SPL 22**	

DATE	DAY	OPPONENT	COMPETITION	SCORE
19 Jan	Sat	**Hearts**	SPL 23	
26 Jan	Sat	St Johnstone	SPL 24	
26/27 Jan	Sat/Sun		League Cup S/F	
30 Jan	**Wed**	**Kilmarnock**	**SPL 25**	
2 Feb	Sat		Scottish Cup R5	
9 Feb	Sat	Inverness CT	SPL 26	
12/13 Feb	Tue/Wed		CL R16	
16 Feb	**Sat**	**Dundee United**	**SPL 27**	
19/20 Feb	Tue/Wed		CL R16	
23 Feb	**Sat**	**Club 12**	**SPL 28**	
27 Feb	Wed	Motherwell	SPL 29	
2 Mar	Sat		Scottish Cup Q/F	
5/6 Mar	Tue/Wed		CL R16	
9 Mar	Sat	Ross County	SPL 30	
12/13	Tue/Wed		CL R16	
16 Mar	**Sat**	**Aberdeen**	**SPL 31**	
17 Mar	Sun		League Cup Final	
30 Mar	Sat	St Mirren	SPL 32	
2/3 Apr	Tue/Wed		CL Q/F	
6 Apr	**Sat**	**Hibernian**	**SPL 33**	
9/10 Apr	Tue/Wed		CL Q/F	
13/14 Apr	Sat/ Sun		Scottish Cup S/F	
20 Apr	Sat		SPL 34	
23/24 Apr	Tue/Wed		CL S/F	
27 Apr	Sat		SPL 35	
30 Apr/1 May	Tue/Wed		CH S/F	
4 May	Sat		SPL 36	
11 May	Sat		SPL 37	
18/19 May	Sat/Sun		SPL 38	
25 May	Sat		CL Final	
26 May	Sun		Scottish Cup Final	
TBA		Dundee United	SPL 2	

All Home games in bold   * All fixture dates and kick-off times subject to change.

CLYDESDALE BANK FIXTURES

SATURDAY, AUGUST 4
Celtic v Aberdeen
Hearts v St Johnstone
Kilmarnock v Club 12
Ross County v Motherwell
St Mirren v Inverness CT

SUNDAY, AUGUST 5
Dundee United v Hibernian

SATURDAY, AUGUST 11
Aberdeen v Ross County
Celtic P-P Dundee United
Club 12 v St Mirren
Hibernian v Hearts
Inverness CT v Kilmarnock
Motherwell v St Johnstone

SATURDAY, AUGUST 18
Dundee United v Club 12
Hearts v Inverness CT
Kilmarnock v Motherwell
Ross County v Celtic
St Johnstone v Aberdeen
St Mirren v Hibernian

SATURDAY, AUGUST 25
Club 12 v Ross County
Hibernian v St Johnstone
Inverness CT v Celtic
Kilmarnock v Dundee United
Motherwell v St Mirren

SUNDAY, AUGUST 26
Aberdeen v Hearts

SATURDAY, SEPTEMBER 1
Aberdeen v St Mirren

Celtic v Hibernian
Motherwell v Inverness CT
Ross County v Kilmarnock
St Johnstone v Dundee United

SUNDAY, SEPTEMBER 2
Hearts v Club 12

SATURDAY, SEPTEMBER 15
Club 12 v Motherwell
Dundee United v Ross County
Hibernian v Kilmarnock
Inverness CT v Aberdeen
St Johnstone v Celtic
St Mirren v Hearts

SATURDAY, SEPTEMBER 22
Aberdeen v Motherwell
Celtic v Club 12
Dundee United v Hearts
Hibernian v Inverness CT
Kilmarnock v St Mirren
Ross County v St Johnstone

SATURDAY, SEPTEMBER 29
Aberdeen v Hibernian
Club 12 v St Johnstone
Hearts v Kilmarnock
Inverness CT v Dundee United
Motherwell v Celtic
St Mirren v Ross County

SATURDAY, OCTOBER 6
Celtic v Hearts
Hibernian v Club 12
Inverness CT v Ross County
Kilmarnock v Aberdeen

2012/13 SEASON

Motherwell v Dundee United
St Johnstone v St Mirren

SATURDAY, OCTOBER 20
Club 12 v Inverness CT
Dundee United v Aberdeen
Hearts v Motherwell
Ross County v Hibernian
St Johnstone v Kilmarnock
St Mirren v Celtic

SATURDAY, OCTOBER 27
Aberdeen v Club 12
Celtic v Kilmarnock
Hearts v Ross County
Inverness CT v St Johnstone
Motherwell v Hibernian
St Mirren v Dundee United

SATURDAY, NOVEMBER 3
Club 12 v Hearts
Dundee United v Celtic
Hibernian v St Mirren
Kilmarnock v Inverness CT
Ross County v Aberdeen
St Johnstone v Motherwell

SATURDAY, NOVEMBER 10
Celtic v St Johnstone
Hibernian v Dundee United
Inverness CT v Hearts
Kilmarnock v Ross County
Motherwell v Club 12
St Mirren v Aberdeen

SATURDAY, NOVEMBER 17
Aberdeen v Celtic

Club 12 v Hibernian
Dundee United v Kilmarnock
Hearts v St Mirren
Inverness CT v Motherwell
St Johnstone v Ross County

SATURDAY, NOVEMBER 24
Celtic v Inverness CT
Hibernian v Aberdeen
Kilmarnock v St Johnstone
Motherwell v Hearts
Ross County v Dundee United
St Mirren v Club 12

WEDNESDAY, NOVEMBER 28
Aberdeen v Inverness CT
Club 12 v Kilmarnock
Dundee United v Motherwell
Hearts v Celtic
Ross County v St Mirren
St Johnstone v Hibernian

SATURDAY, DECEMBER 8
Club 12 v Dundee United
Hearts v Aberdeen
Inverness CT v Hibernian
Kilmarnock v Celtic
Motherwell v Ross County
St Mirren v St Johnstone

SATURDAY, DECEMBER 15
Aberdeen v Kilmarnock
Celtic v St Mirren
Dundee United v Inverness CT
Hibernian v Motherwell
Ross County v Club 12
St Johnstone v Hearts

CLYDESDALE BANK FIXTURES

SATURDAY, DECEMBER 22
Aberdeen v St Johnstone
Celtic v Ross County
Hearts v Dundee United
Inverness CT v Club 12
Kilmarnock v Hibernian
St Mirren v Motherwell

WEDNESDAY, DECEMBER 26
Club 12 v Celtic
Dundee United v St Johnstone
Hibernian v Ross County
Inverness CT v St Mirren
Kilmarnock v Hearts
Motherwell v Aberdeen

SATURDAY, DECEMBER 29
Club 12 v Aberdeen
Dundee United v St Mirren
Hibernian v Celtic
Motherwell v Kilmarnock
Ross County v Hearts
St Johnstone v Inverness CT

WEDNESDAY, JANUARY 2
Aberdeen v Dundee United
Celtic v Motherwell
Hearts v Hibernian
Ross County v Inverness CT
St Johnstone v Club 12
St Mirren v Kilmarnock

SATURDAY, JANUARY 19
Celtic v Hearts
Hibernian v Club 12
Inverness CT v Aberdeen
Kilmarnock v Dundee United

Motherwell v St Johnstone
St Mirren v Ross County

SATURDAY, JANUARY 26
Aberdeen v Hibernian
Club 12 v St Mirren
Dundee United v Ross County
Hearts v Motherwell
Inverness CT v Kilmarnock
St Johnstone v Celtic

WEDNESDAY, JANUARY 30
Celtic v Kilmarnock
Hearts v Club 12
Motherwell v Dundee United
Ross County v Hibernian
St Johnstone v Aberdeen
St Mirren v Inverness CT

SATURDAY, FEBRUARY 9
Aberdeen v St Mirren
Club 12 v Ross County
Dundee United v Hearts
Hibernian v St Johnstone
Inverness CT v Celtic
Kilmarnock v Motherwell

SATURDAY, FEBRUARY 16
Aberdeen v Club 12
Celtic v Dundee United
Hearts v Kilmarnock
Motherwell v Inverness CT
Ross County v St Johnstone
St Mirren v Hibernian

SATURDAY, FEBRUARY 23
Celtic v Club 12
Dundee United v Hibernian

2012/13 SEASON

Hearts v Inverness CT
Kilmarnock v Aberdeen
Ross County v Motherwell
St Johnstone v St Mirren

Hearts v St Johnstone
Inverness CT v Ross County
Kilmarnock v St Mirren
Motherwell v Hibernian

WEDNESDAY, FEBRUARY 27
Aberdeen v Ross County
Club 12 v St Johnstone
Hibernian v Kilmarnock
Inverness CT v Dundee United
Motherwell v Celtic
St Mirren v Hearts

SATURDAY, MARCH 30
Aberdeen v Hearts
Club 12 v Motherwell
Hibernian v Inverness CT
Ross County v Kilmarnock
St Johnstone v Dundee United
St Mirren v Celtic

SATURDAY, MARCH 9
Aberdeen v Motherwell
Club 12 v Inverness CT
Hibernian v Hearts
Ross County v Celtic
St Johnstone v Kilmarnock
St Mirren v Dundee United

SATURDAY, APRIL 6
Celtic v Hibernian
Dundee United v Aberdeen
Hearts v Ross County
Inverness CT v St Johnstone
Kilmarnock v Club 12
Motherwell v St Mirren

SATURDAY, MARCH 16
Celtic v Aberdeen
Dundee United v Club 12

* All fixture dates and kick-off
times subject to change.

ABERDEEN

Founded: 1903
Stadium: Pittodrie
Capacity: 22,199
Nickname: The Dons
Manager: Craig Brown

Website: www.afc.co.uk
Telephone: 01224 650400
Email: feedback@afc.co.uk

COLOURS:
(Home)	*(Away)*
Red shirts	*White shirts*
Red shorts	*White shorts*
Red socks	*White socks*

HONOURS

LEAGUE CHAMPIONSHIP (4)
1954/55; 1979/80; 1983/84; 1984/85

SCOTTISH CUP (7)
1947, 1970, 1982, 1983, 1984, 1986, 1990

LEAGUE CUP (5)
1955/56; 1976/77; 1985/86; 1989/90; 1995/96

EUROPEAN CUP-WINNERS' CUP
1983

EUROPEAN SUPER CUP
1983/84

DID YOU KNOW?
It was Dumbarton-born, Donald Colman, a former Aberdeen player who, when coaching with the club came up with the idea of a dugout to keep his eyes on the players' feet – and so, Pittodrie in the 1930s was the first stadium to feature what is now an accepted part of every football ground.

RECORD V CELTIC

	Celtic wins	Draws	Aberdeen wins
League	138	61	65
Scottish Cup	14	7	8
League Cup	14	4	9
TOTAL	**166**	**72**	**82**

FIRST GAME V CELTIC
December 9, 1905 (League)
Celtic 1-0 Aberdeen

BIGGEST VICTORY V CELTIC
August 17, 1946
Aberdeen 6-2 Celtic

BIGGEST DEFEAT V CELTIC
November 6, 2010
Celtic 9-0 Aberdeen

RESULTS LAST SEASON:
SPL: 07/08/11
Aberdeen 0-1 Celtic
SPL: 23/10/11
Celtic 2-1 Aberdeen
SPL: 03/03/12
Aberdeen 1-1 Celtic

2012/13 FIXTURES V CELTIC

SPL: Celtic v Aberdeen 04/06/12
SPL: Aberdeen v Celtic 17/11/12
SPL: Celtic v Aberdeen 16/03/13

CLUB 12

*THE fixtures for season 2012/13 were released
on Monday, June 18 and they included a
CLUB 12 in the fixture list.*

*The SPL explained that "Following the failure
of Rangers FC to exit administration via a CVA,
we have received an application to register the
transfer of their SPL share to a newco. Should it
be rejected, then another club may be invited to
join the SPL for season 2012/13."*

2012/13 FIXTURES V CELTIC

SPL: Celtic v Club 12 22/09/12
SPL: Club 12 v Celtic 26/12/12
SPL: Celtic v Club 12 23/02/13

DUNDEE UNITED

Founded: 1909
Stadium: Tannadice
Capacity: 14,209
Nickname: The Terrors
Manager: Peter Houston

Website: www.dundeeunitedfc.co.uk
Telephone: 01382 833166
Email: enquiries@dundeeunitedfc.co.uk

COLOURS:
(Home)   *(Away)*
Tangerine shirts   *White & Black shirts*
Black shorts   *White shorts*
Tangerine socks   *White socks*

HONOURS

LEAGUE CHAMPIONSHIP (1)
1982/83

SCOTTISH CUP (2)
1994, 2010

LEAGUE CUP (2)
1979/80, 1980/81

DID YOU KNOW?
It's not uncommon for weather to interrupt the football schedule at one end of the country and not the other – but what about both ends of the same street? In 1947, snow made Tannadice unplayable for United's League Cup tie against Rangers but, 170 yards up the street at Dens Park the pitch was playable and that's where the game went ahead!

RECORD V DUNDEE UNITED

	Celtic wins	Draws	Dundee Utd wins
League	98	44	34
Scottish Cup	12	1	2
League Cup	14	6	5
TOTAL	**124**	**51**	**41**

FIRST GAME V CELTIC
September 19, 1925 (League)
Dundee United 0-1 Celtic

BIGGEST VICTORY V CELTIC
Dundee United 3-0 Celtic (1962/63;
1979/80; 1981/82' 1985/86)

BIGGEST DEFEAT V CELTIC
March 1, 1930
Celtic 7-0 Dundee United

RESULTS LAST SEASON:
SPL: 13/08/11
Celtic 5-1 Dundee United
SPL: 04/12/11
Dundee United 0-1 Celtic
SPL: 14/01/12
Celtic 2-1 Dundee United
Scottish Cup: 11/03/12
Dundee United 0-4 Celtic
SPL: 06/05/12
Dundee United 1-0 Celtic

2012/13 FIXTURES V CELTIC

SPL: Celtic v Dundee United TBA
SPL: Dundee United v Celtic 03/11/12
SPL: Celtic v Dundee United 16/02/13

HEART OF MIDLOTHIAN

Founded: 1874
Stadium: Tynecastle
Capacity: 17,420
Nickname: The Jambos
Manager: TBC

Website: www.heartsfc.co.uk
Telephone: 0871 663 1874
Email: Details via website

COLOURS:
(Home)
Maroon shirts
White shorts
Maroon socks

(Away)
Navy/Beetroot shirts
Navy shorts
Navy socks

HONOURS

LEAGUE CHAMPIONSHIP (4)
1894/95, 1896/97, 1957/58,
1959/60

SCOTTISH CUP (8)
1891, 1896, 1901, 1906, 1956,
1998, 2006, 2012

LEAGUE CUP (4)
1954/55, 1958/59, 1959/60,
1962/63

DID YOU KNOW?
The man who wrote the Tynecastle anthem, The Hearts Song also wrote Glory, Glory to the Hibees for Hibs, The Terrors of Tannadice for Dundee United and Dark Blue of Dundee for Dundee. The songsmith with the multicoloured pen was old comedian Hector Nicol – who came from Paisley and supported St Mirren!

RECORD V CELTIC

	Celtic wins	Draws	Hearts wins
League	151	66	70
Scottish Cup	17	5	6
League Cup	12	1	7
TOTAL	**180**	**72**	**83**

FIRST GAME V CELTIC
August 23, 1890 (League)
Hearts 0-5 Celtic

BIGGEST VICTORY V CELTIC
September 14, 1895
Celtic 0-5 Hearts

BIGGEST DEFEATS V CELTIC
April 20, 1908 & April 1, 1981
Celtic 6-0 Hearts

RESULTS LAST SEASON:
SPL: 02/10/11
Hearts 2-0 Celtic
SPL: 10/12/11
Celtic 1-0 Hearts
SPL: 08/02/12
Hearts 0-4 Celtic
Scottish Cup: 15/04/12
Celtic 1-2 Hearts
SPL: 13/05/12
Celtic 5-0 Hearts

2012/13 FIXTURES V CELTIC

SPL: Celtic v Hearts 06/10/12
SPL: Hearts v Celtic 28/11/12
SPL: Celtic v Hearts 19/01/13

HIBERNIAN

Founded: 1875
Stadium: Easter Road
Capacity: 20,421
Nickname: The Hibees
Manager: Pat Fenlon

Website: www.hibernianfc.co.uk
Telephone: 0131 661 2159
Email: club@hibernianfc.co.uk

COLOURS:
(Home)
Green and white shirts
White shorts
Green socks

(Away)
Mint shirts
Mint shorts
Black socks

HONOURS

LEAGUE CHAMPIONSHIP (4)
1902/03, 1947/48, 1950/51,
1951/52

SCOTTISH CUP (2)
1887, 1902

LEAGUE CUP (3)
1972/73, 1991/92, 2006/07

DID YOU KNOW?
The very first game European Cup game played in Glasgow featured Hibernian when they lost 1-0 to Swedish side Djurgardens IF in the second-round of the inaugural 1955/56 competition after winning 3-1 at Easter Road. Because of the weather in Sweden at the time, the Scandinavian side played their 'home' game at Firhill.

RECORD V CELTIC

	Celtic wins	Draws	Hibernian wins
League	162	65	50
Scottish Cup	13	7	3
League Cup	11	5	6
TOTAL	**186**	**77**	**59**

FIRST GAME V CELTIC
December 29, 1894
Hibernian 0-2 Celtic

BIGGEST VICTORY V CELTIC
September 14, 1895
Celtic 0-5 Hibernian

BIGGEST DEFEAT V CELTIC
Celtic 6-0 Hibernian (1930/31;
1960/61; 1981/82; 2003/04)

RESULTS LAST SEASON:
SPL: 24/07/11
Hibernian 0-2 Celtic
League Cup: 26/10/11
Hibernian 1-4 Celtic
SPL: 29/10/11
Celtic 0-0 Hibernian
SPL: 19/02/12
Hibernian 0-5 Celtic

2012/13 FIXTURES V CELTIC

SPL: Celtic v Hibernian 01/09/12
SPL: Hibernian v Celtic 29/12/12
SPL: Celtic v Hibernian 06/04/13

INVERNESS CALEDONIAN THISTLE

Founded: 1994
Stadium: Caledonian Stadium
Capacity: 7,819
Nickname: Caley Thistle
Manager: Terry Butcher

Website: www.ictfc.co.uk
Telephone: 01463 222880
Email: tickets@ictfc.co.uk

COLOURS:
(Home)
Red and Blue Striped Shirts
Blue shorts
Blue socks

(Away)
White shirts
Red shorts
Red socks

HONOURS

NO MAJOR HONOURS

DID YOU KNOW?
When Inverness CT first played in the top tier, their stadium didn't meet SPL criteria so they ground-shared with nearest 'neighbours' Aberdeen. But for players and fans, every home game meant a two-and-a-half hour journey to Pittodrie and a round trip of around 210 miles.

RECORD V CELTIC

	Celtic wins	Draws	Inverness wins
League	15	4	2
Scottish Cup	3	0	2
League Cup	2	0	0
TOTAL	**20**	**4**	**4**

FIRST GAME V CELTIC
February 8, 2000 (Scottish Cup)
Celtic 1-3 Inverness CT

BIGGEST VICTORY V CELTIC
February 8, 2000 (Scottish Cup)
Celtic 1-3 Inverness CT

BIGGEST DEFEAT V CELTIC
September 22, 2010 (League Cup)
Celtic 6-0 Inverness CT

RESULTS LAST SEASON:
SPL: 24/09/11
Celtic 2-0 Inverness CT
SPL: 19/11/11
Inverness CT 0-2 Celtic
Scottish Cup: 04/02/12
Inverness CT 0-2 Celtic
SPL: 11/05/12
Celtic 1-0 Inverness CT

2012/13 FIXTURES V CELTIC

SPL: Inverness CT v Celtic 25/08/12
SPL: Celtic v Inverness CT 24/11/12
SPL: Inverness CT v Celtic 09/02/13

KILMARNOCK

Founded: 1869
Stadium: Rugby Park
Capacity: 18,128
Nickname: Killie
Manager: Kenny Shiels

Website: www.kilmarnockfc.co.uk
Telephone: 01563 545300
Email: tickets@kilmarnockfc.co.uk

COLOURS:
(Home)	(Away)
Blue and White striped shirts	Yellow shirts
Blue shorts	Yellow shorts
Blue socks	Yellow socks

HONOURS

LEAGUE CHAMPIONSHIP (1)
1964/65

SCOTTISH CUP (3)
1920, 1929, 1997

LEAGUE CUP (1)
2011/12

DID YOU KNOW?
Rugby Park is Kilmarnock's fourth ground and it was Celtic who scored the first ever goal there when it was opened on August 26, 1899. The last ever game played at the stadium before it was re-built was on May 7, 1994 when Killie beat Rangers 1-0.

RECORD V CELTIC

	Celtic wins	Draws	Kilmarnock wins
League	138	43	26
Scottish Cup	11	3	5
League Cup	6	2	2
TOTAL	**155**	**48**	**33**

FIRST GAME V CELTIC
August 26, 1899 (League)
Kilmarnock 2-2 Celtic

BIGGEST VICTORY V CELTIC
March 27, 1963
Kilmarnock 6-0 Celtic

BIGGEST DEFEAT V CELTIC
August 13, 1938
Celtic 9-1 Kilmarnock

RESULTS LAST SEASON:
SPL: 15/10/11
Kilmarnock 3-3 Celtic
SPL: 24/12/11
Celtic 2-1 Kilmarnock
League Cup: 18/03/12
Kilmarnock 1-0 Celtic
SPL: 07/04/12
Kilmarnock 0-6 Celtic

2012/13 FIXTURES V CELTIC

SPL: Celtic v Kilmarnock 27/10/12
SPL: Kilmarnock v Celtic 08/12/12
SPL: Celtic v Kilmarnock 30/01/13

MOTHERWELL

Founded: 1886
Stadium: Fir Park
Capacity: 13,742
Nickname: The Steelmen
Manager: Stuart McCall

Website: www.motherwellfc.co.uk
Telephone: 01698 333333
Email: mfc@motherwellfc.co.uk

COLOURS:
(Home)
Claret & Amber shirts
Claret shorts
Claret socks

(Away)
White shirts
White shorts
White socks

HONOURS

LEAGUE CHAMPIONSHIP (1)
1931/32

SCOTTISH CUP (2)
1952, 1991

LEAGUE CUP (1)
1950/51

DID YOU KNOW?
Motherwell, who originally wore blue and white, made the change to claret and amber in 1913 and the first design was basically the same as that of Bradford City who were operating in the top flight down south at the time.

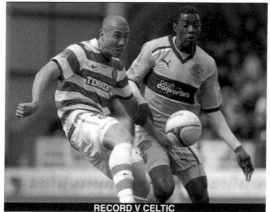

RECORD V CELTIC

	Celtic wins	Draws	Motherwell wins
League	152	54	46
Scottish Cup	16	8	5
League Cup	10	3	3
TOTAL	**178**	**65**	**54**

FIRST GAME V CELTIC
January 16, 1904 (League)
Celtic 6-0 Motherwell

BIGGEST VICTORY V CELTIC
April 30, 1937
Motherwell 8-0 Celtic

BIGGEST DEFEAT V CELTIC
September 18, 1982
Celtic 7-0 Motherwell

RESULTS LAST SEASON:
SPL: 10/09/11
Celtic 4-0 Motherwell
SPL: 06/11/11
Motherwell 1-2 Celtic
SPL: 25/02/12
Celtic 1-0 Motherwell
SPL: 22/04/12
Motherwell 0-3 Celtic

2012/13 FIXTURES V CELTIC

SPL: Motherwell v Celtic 29/09/12
SPL: Celtic v Motherwell 02/01/13
SPL: Motherwell v Celtic 27/02/13

ROSS COUNTY

Founded: 1929
Stadium: Victoria Park
Capacity: 6,310
Nickname: The Staggies
Manager: Derek Adams

Website: www.rosscountyfootballclub.co.uk
Telephone: 01349 860860
Email: Details via website

COLOURS:
(Home)   *(Away)*
Blue shirts with white flash   *White shirts with red trim*
Blue shorts   *White shorts*
Blue socks   *White socks with red trim*

HONOURS

NO MAJOR HONOURS

DID YOU KNOW?
Ross County have won the First, Second and Third Division titles
once each since 1999 and prior to joining the senior set-up they lifted
the Highland League title on three occasions.

RECORD V CELTIC

	Celtic wins	Draws	Ross County wins
League	0	0	0
Scottish Cup	1	0	1
League Cup	1	0	0
TOTAL	**2**	**0**	**1**

FIRST GAME V CELTIC
January 10, 2004 (Scottish Cup)
Celtic 2-0 Ross County

RESULTS LAST SEASON:
League Cup: 21/09/12
Ross County 0-2 Celtic

BIGGEST VICTORY V CELTIC
April 10, 2011
Ross County 2-0 Celtic

BIGGEST DEFEAT V CELTIC
Celtic 2-0 Ross County
(2004 & 2011)

2012/13 FIXTURES V CELTIC

SPL: Ross County v Celtic 18/08/12
SPL: Celtic v Ross County 22/12/12
SPL: Ross County v Celtic 09/03/13

ST JOHNSTONE

Founded: 1884
Stadium: McDiarmid Park
Capacity: 10,456
Nickname: The Saints
Manager: Steve Lomas

Website: www.perthstjohnstonefc.co.uk
Telephone: 01738 459090
Email: enquiries@perthsaints.co.uk

COLOURS:
(Home)	*(Away)*
Blue shirts	*White shirts*
White shorts	*White shorts*
Blue socks	*White socks*

HONOURS

NO MAJOR HONOURS

DID YOU KNOW?
St Johnstone were managed by Bobby Brown from 1958 until 1967 who was then succeeded by Willie Ormond who was there from 1967 until 1973 – both men left the Saints to take up the position of Scotland manager.

RECORD V CELTIC

	Celtic wins	Draws	St Johnstone wins
League	70	18	18
Scottish Cup	5	0	1
League Cup	4	0	3
TOTAL	**79**	**18**	**22**

FIRST GAME V CELTIC
October 18, 1924 (League)
St Johnstone 0-0 Celtic

BIGGEST VICTORY V CELTIC
November 7, 1964
St Johnstone 3-0 Celtic

BIGGEST DEFEAT V CELTIC
October 23, 1937
Celtic 6-0 St Johnstone

RESULTS LAST SEASON:
SPL: 21/08/11
Celtic 0-1 St Johnstone
SPL: 18/12/11
St Johnstone 0-2 Celtic
SPL: 01/04/12
Celtic 2-0 St Johnstone
SPL: 03/05/12
Celtic 1-0 St Johnstone

2012/13 FIXTURES V CELTIC

SPL: St Johnstone v Celtic 15/09/12
SPL: Celtic v St Johnstone 10/11/12
SPL: St Johnstone v Celtic 26/01/13

ST MIRREN

Founded: 1877
Stadium: St Mirren Park
Capacity: 8,023
Nickname: The Buddies
Manager: Danny Lennon

Website: www.saintmirren.org
Telephone: 0141 889 2558
Email: info@stmirren.net

COLOURS:
(Home)
Black & White striped shirts
White shorts
Black & White socks

(Away)
Red & Black striped shirts
Red shorts
Red & Black socks

HONOURS

SCOTTISH CUP (3)
1926, 1959, 1987

DID YOU KNOW?
Before the Camp Nou, there was the Camp de Les Corts which Barcelona opened as their new ground in 1922 with a game against St Mirren. It was a tournament to open Barca's new home and the Saints beat Notts County in the final.

RECORD V CELTIC

	Celtic wins	Draws	St Mirren wins
League	157	38	30
Scottish Cup	16	7	6
League Cup	11	0	3
TOTAL	**184**	**45**	**39**

FIRST GAME V CELTIC
February 7, 1891 (League)
Celtic 3-2 St Mirren

BIGGEST VICTORY V CELTIC
October 1, 1898
St Mirren 4-0 Celtic

BIGGEST DEFEAT V CELTIC
Celtic 7-0 St Mirren
(1962/63; 1980/81; 2008/09)

RESULTS LAST SEASON:
SPL: 28/08/11
St Mirren 0-2 Celtic
SPL: 26/11/11
Celtic 5-0 St Mirren
SPL: 21/01/12
St Mirren 0-2 Celtic

2011/12 FIXTURES V CELTIC

SPL: St Mirren v Celtic 20/10/12
SPL: Celtic v St Mirren 15/12/12
SPL: St Mirren v Celtic 30/03/13

SCOTTISH FIRST DIVISION

TEAM	STADIUM
Ayr United	Somerset Park
Cowdenbeath	Central Park
Dundee	Dens Park
Dunfermline Athletic	East End Park
Falkirk	Falkirk Stadium
Morton	Cappielow
Hamilton	New Douglas Park
Livingston	Braidwood Stadium
Partick Thistle	Firhill
Raith Rovers	Starks Park

SCOTTISH SECOND DIVISION

TEAM	STADIUM
Airdrie United	New Broomfield
Albion Rovers	Cliftonhill
Alloa Athletic	Recreation Park
Arbroath	Gayfield Park
Brechin City	Glebe Park
Dumbarton	Strathclyde Homes Stadium
East Fife	New Bayview Stadium
Forfar Athletic	Station Park
Queen of the South	Palmertson Park
Stenhousemuir	Ochilview Park

SCOTTISH THIRD DIVISION

TEAM	STADIUM
Annan Athletic	Galabank
Berwick Rangers	Shielfield Park
Clyde	Broadwood
East Stirling	Ochilview Park
Elgin City	Borough Briggs
Montrose	Links Park
Peterhead	Balmoor
Queen's Park	Hampden Park
Stirling Albion	Doubletree Dunblane Stadium
Stranraer	Stair Park

CAPACITY	KIT COLOURS
10,243	White & Black
4,370	Blue & White
12,085	Dark Blue
12,509	Black & White
9,120	Navy Blue
11,612	Blue & White Hoops
6,096	Red & White Hoops
10,122	Gold & Black
10,887	Yellow & Red
10,104	Navy Blue

CAPACITY	KIT COLOURS
10,170	White & Red Diamond
2,496	Yellow
3,142	Black & Gold Hoops
4,125	Maroon
3,960	Red & White
2,020	Gold
1,992	Gold & Black
5,177	Blue & Black
6,412	Blue
2,654	Maroon

CAPACITY	KIT COLOURS
500	Black & Gold
4,131	Black & Gold
8,029	White
2,654	Black
4,962	Black & White
3,292	Blue
4,500	Blue
52,046	Black & White Hoops
3,808	Red
6,100	Blue

STADIUM TOURS

GET INSIDE AN EXCLUSIVE BEHIND THE SCENES INSIGHT INTO CELTIC FOOTBALL CLUB

Adults £8.50, Concessions £5.50 Family Ticket £20 (2 adults and 2 children or 1 adult and 3 children) Under 5's are admitted free.

TO BOOK YOUR PLACE PLEASE CONTACT

CALL > **0871 226 1888***
EMAIL > **STADIUMTOURS@CELTICFC.CO.UK**

FIRST
TEAM

CELTIC MANAGEMENT TEAM

NEIL LENNON

While the players have made heroes of themselves over the last two seasons, it's Neil Lennon who is the real fans' favourite. He became a Celtic legend during his playing days at the club, and is becoming just as successful as a manager too. He signed for Celtic in December 2000 and went on to win five SPL titles, three Scottish Cups, two League Cups and reached the final of the UEFA Cup. He also captained the side for his last two seasons in Glasgow. He moved to England to finish his playing career but returned to Celtic to work with the Development Squad after he took up coaching.

In March 2010 he took temporary charge of the manager's role after Tony Mowbray left, and the position was made permanent three months later. As the gaffer, he promised the Celtic support he would bring the thunder back to Paradise and that is exactly what he has done, winning the Scottish Cup in 2011 and the league title the following year.

JOHAN MJALLBY

Johan Mjallby was an absolute rock in defence during his playing days and never let the side down. He made his debut for Celtic in the 5-1 win against Rangers in 1998 and never looked back, winning seven trophies in his six years at the club.

The Swede also won 49 caps for his country and scored in the opening match of Euro 2000. He left the Hoops in 2004 and bowed out quietly due to a calf injury. Neil Lennon appointed him as his temporary assistant manager in March 2010 and along with the other coaches, his post became permanent three months later.

GARRY PARKER

As a former Leicester City team-mate of Neil Lennon's, Parker joined the Celtic coaching set-up when it all changed in 2010. During his playing days he enjoyed spells at Luton Town, Hull City, Nottingham Forest and Aston Villa, where he played in midfield. He also earned six under-21 caps for England and one for the B team. He was appointed caretaker manager of Leicester City in 2001 but then after a period out of the game he took on the role at Celtic.

STEVIE WOODS

Before Stevie Woods took over as Head Goalkeeping Coach at Celtic, most fans knew him from his playing days at Motherwell. He was there for almost a decade and came up against Celtic numerous times during the late 1990s and in the Martin O'Neill era. He came through Hibernian's youth academy before starting his career at Clydebank in 1992. After hanging up his boots in 2006, he coached at Dunfermline before moving to Celtic two years later.

CELTIC FC

No.24 LUKASZ ZALUSKA
POSITION: Goalkeeper
DATE OF BIRTH: 16/06/82
BORN: Wysokie Mazowieckie, Poland
HEIGHT: 6'4"

PREVIOUS CLUBS:
Dundee United, Korona Kielce, Legia Warsaw, Stomil Olsztyn, Zryw Zielona Gora, Sparta Obornoki, MSP Szamotuly, Ruch Wysokie Mazowieckie

CELTIC DEBUT: *v Falkirk (a) 4-0, League Cup, 23/09/09*

APPEARANCES:
League: 17 + 1 sub
League Cup: 2
Scottish Cup: 5 + 2 sub
Europe: 7
TOTAL: 31 + 3 sub

The Polish internationalist moved to Scotland in 2007 when he signed for Dundee United - and it was his performances there which caught Celtic's attention. He signed a pre-contract with the Hoops in January 2009 and shortly after took part in the 11-10 penalty shoot-out, in the Scottish Cup, against his new club – and even scored from the spot himself. He started last season in goal until Fraser Forster's arrival but even though he wasn't a regular in the starting XI, the Polish keeper showed his dedication to the club by signing a new three-and-a-half year deal in March 2012.

CELTIC FC

ROBBIE THOMSON
POSITION: Goalkeeper
DATE OF BIRTH: 07/03/93
BORN: Glasgow, Scotland
HEIGHT: 6'0"

CELTIC DEBUT: *n/a*

The son of former Dunfermline keeper, Scott Thomson, Robbie has followed in his father's footsteps and pulled on the gloves. He has worked his way through the ranks at Celtic, learning his trade between the sticks. Nick Feely's return from injury pushed him down the pecking order in the latter stages of the 2010/11 season but with the Australian progressing up to the Development Squad, Thomson's final year at 19s' level saw him occupy the goals. And injury kept him out in early 2012 but he returned for the Youth Cup final in April.

CELTIC FC

No.2 ADAM MATTHEWS
POSITION: Central defence
DATE OF BIRTH: 13/01/92
BORN: Swansea
HEIGHT: 5'10"

PREVIOUS CLUBS:
Cardiff City

CELTIC DEBUT: *v Aberdeen (a) 1-0,
Scottish Premier League, 07/08/11*

APPEARANCES:
*League: 25 + 2 sub
League Cup: 3 + 1 sub
Scottish Cup: 2
Europe: 4
TOTAL: 34 + 3 sub*

Matthews was just 19-years-old when he signed for
Celtic in the summer of 2011 but despite his youth he
managed to establish himself as a first-team regular
over the course of the season. He took advantage of
Mark Wilson's three-month injury lay-off and impressed
in the right-back role. His has also become a regular on
the international stage as well, after making his debut
for Wales against Scotland in May 2011. The defender is
a mature and composed player and has a bright future
ahead of him.

CELTIC FC

No.3 EMILIO IZAGUIRRE
POSITION: Left-back
DATE OF BIRTH: 10/05/86
BORN: Honduras
HEIGHT: 5'8"

PREVIOUS CLUBS:
Montagua

CELTIC DEBUT: *v Motherwell (a) 1-0,*
Scottish Premier League, 29/08/10

APPEARANCES:	GOALS:
League: 43 + 3 subs	*League: 1*
League Cup: 5	*TOTAL: 1*
Scottish Cup: 6	
TOTAL: 53 + 3 subs	

The Honduran internationalist caught Celtic's eye during the 2010 World Cup in South Africa but still arrived in Scotland as a largely unknown quantity. He put amends to that almost instantly, lighting up Scottish football with his fancy footwork and exciting ability to attack from the full-back position. He lifted every Player of the Year award available at the end of season 2010/11 but just three weeks into the new campaign he suffered a devastating ankle break. Charlie Mulgrew and Joe Ledley provided cover for the left-back position until he returned in January and he gradually eased his way back into the championship-winning side.

CELTIC FC

No.6 Kelvin Wilson
POSITION: Central defence
DATE OF BIRTH: 03/09/85
BORN: Nottingham
HEIGHT: 6'2"

PREVIOUS CLUBS:
Nottingham Forest, Preston North End, Notts County

CELTIC DEBUT: *v Hibernian (a) 2-0,*
Scottish Premier League, 24/06/11

APPEARANCES:
League: 13 + 1 sub
League Cup: 2
Scottish Cup: 3
Europe: 2
TOTAL: 20 + 1 sub

The central-defender was Neil Lennon's first signing of
summer 2011, making the move from his boyhood heroes,
Nottingham Forest. He played for the Championship side
for four years, following spells at Preston, and Notts County
where he turned professional. He became a first-team
regular at Celtic almost instantly but went on to miss three
months with an Achilles injury. He managed to get back
into the fold, however, and seized his chance after Daniel
Majstorovic tore a knee ligament.

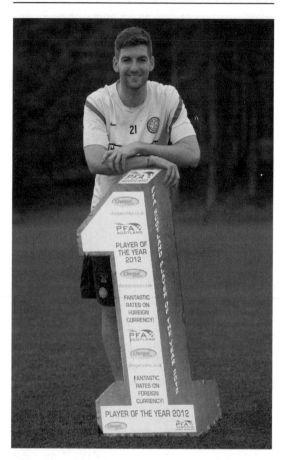

CELTIC FC

No.21 CHARLIE MULGREW
POSITION: Defender/Midfielder
DATE OF BIRTH: 06/03/86
BORN: Glasgow
HEIGHT: 6'2"

PREVIOUS CLUBS:
Celtic, Dundee United (loan), Wolves,
Southend (loan), Aberdeen

CELTIC DEBUT: *v SC Braga (a) 0-3,*
UEFA Champions League qualifier, 28/07/10

APPEARANCES:	GOALS:
League: 49 + 4 sub	*League: 8*
League Cup: 5 + 2 sub	*League Cup: 1*
Scottish Cup: 10	*Scottish Cup: 2*
Europe: 8 + 1 sub	*Europe: 1*
TOTAL: 72 + 7 sub	*TOTAL: 12*

Mulgrew was handed a second opportunity at Celtic when Neil Lennon brought the former Youth Academy graduate back to the club in 2010. He took a while to settle into the side, but halfway through the season he emerged as one of the squad's key players. And he continued where he left off at the start of the 2011/12 campaign which, by the end of, he had lifted every Player of the Year award on offer. The defender switched between left-back, in Emilio Izaguirre's absence, and centre-half, where he was outstanding, but also contributed with his fair share of goals and assists throughout the season as well. He also topped off his incredible run of form with his first Scotland call-up in February, 2012.

CELTIC FC

No.23 MIKAEL LUSTIG
POSITION: Right-back
DATE OF BIRTH: 13/12/86
BORN: Umea, Sweden
HEIGHT: 6'3"

PREVIOUS CLUBS:
Sandakerms SK, Umea, GIF Sundsvall, Rosenborg

CELTIC DEBUT: *v Aberdeen (a) 1-1,*
Scottish Premier League, 03/03/12

APPEARANCES:
League: 3 + 1 sub
Scottish Cup: 1
TOTAL: 4 + 1 sub

The defender established himself in his homeland, Sweden,
before making the move to Norway, where he joined
Rosenborg. Lustig signed for Celtic during the January 2012
transfer window but was unfortunate to pick up an injury not
long into his Celtic career. He worked his way through rehab,
though, and made his debut against Aberdeen, at Pittodrie,
at the start of March. He has been a full internationalist for
four years now and was also one of Celtic's representatives
at Euro 2012.

CELTIC FC

No.25 THOMAS ROGNE

POSITION: Defender
DATE OF BIRTH: 29/06/90
BORN: Baerum, Norway
HEIGHT: 6'4"

PREVIOUS CLUBS:
Stabaek

CELTIC DEBUT: *v Hearts (h) 2-0,*
Scottish Premier League, 10/02/10

APPEARANCES:	GOALS:
League: 32 + 5 sub	*League: 2*
League Cup: 5	*League Cup: 1*
Scottish Cup: 4	*TOTAL: 3*
TOTAL: 41 + 5 sub	

When Rogne signed for Celtic in January 2010, he came to Scotland with the reputation of being one of Norway's rising stars. However, niggling injuries hampered any early hopes of making the team immediately. But, he excelled in the second-half of the 2011/12 campaign and after getting a consistent run in the team he settled into the centre of defence well. He became a key part of the starting XI, especially following Daniel Majstorovic's injury, and showed how reliable he is under pressure. His hard work was also rewarded with his first international cap for Norway's senior side in February 2012.

CELTIC FC

No.39 ANDRE BLACKMAN
POSITION: Defender
DATE OF BIRTH: 10/11/90
BORN: London, England
HEIGHT: 6'0"
PREVIOUS CLUBS:
AFC Wimbledon, Bristol City

CELTIC DEBUT: v Aberdeen (a) 1-1,
Scottish Premier League, 10/09/12

APPEARANCES:
League: 1 + 2 sub
TOTAL: 1 + 2 sub

The young left-back was offered a contract until the end
of the campaign after he impressed during a trial period in
November. The Londoner had been without a club since
leaving AFC Wimbledon in the summer, having being on
the books of Arsenal, Chelsea and Spurs at one stage. He
also includes Portsmouth and Bristol City among his former
clubs. Was unfortunate when the ball deflected off him for
Aberdeen's goal in the 1-1 draw on his debut.

CELTIC FC

No.45 LEWIS TOSHNEY
POSITION: Defender
DATE OF BIRTH: 26/04/92
BORN: Dundee, Scotland
HEIGHT: 5'11"

PREVIOUS CLUBS:
Kilmarnock (loan)

CELTIC DEBUT: *v Aberdeen (a) 3-0,*
Scottish Premier League, 01/02/11

APPEARANCES:
League: 1 sub
TOTAL: 1 sub

Toshney joined the Hoops at 12-years-old and has
progressed all the way up to the Development Squad. He
returned from injury in the 2010/11 season and stood in as
captain for most of their double-winning season. Due to
injuries at the start of 2011, Toshney made his debut for the
first-team against Aberdeen, coming on as a substitute. But
in order to gain experience he moved to Kilmarnock on loan
for the second-half of the 2011/12 season where he became a
regular in the side.

CELTIC FC

No.44 MARCUS FRASER
POSITION: Defender
DATE OF BIRTH: 23/06/94
BORN: Scotland
HEIGHT: 5'11"

CELTIC DEBUT: *v Rennes (h) 3-1,*
UEFA Europa League, 03/11/11

APPEARANCES:
Europe: 1 sub
TOTAL: 1 sub

Marcus Fraser impressed so much at youth level it
ultimately led to a greater involvement with the Under-19s
at the age of 16. Shortly after representing Scotland's
U17s in March 2011, he travelled to Bilbao with the Celtic
first-team for a friendly. He made an appearance that
evening and continued to stay in Neil Lennon's plans.
Building on this, he made his competitive debut at
first-team level in November 2011, coming on as a
half-time substitute in the UEFA Europa League match
against Rennes, with the Hoops winning 3-1.

CELTIC FC

No.8 SCOTT BROWN
POSITION: Midfielder
DATE OF BIRTH: 25/06/85
BORN: Dunfermline, Scotland
HEIGHT: 5'9"

PREVIOUS CLUBS:
Hibernian

CELTIC DEBUT: *v Kilmarnock (h) 0-0,
Scottish Premier League, 05/08/07*

APPEARANCES:	GOALS:
League: 132 + 9 sub	*League: 14*
League Cup: 9 + 1 sub	*League Cup: 2*
Scottish Cup: 16 + 1 sub	*Scottish Cup: 4*
Europe: 27 + 2 sub	*TOTAL: 20*
TOTAL: 184 + 13 sub	

Brown made a name for himself at Hibernian in a very
talented side and as a result attracted attention from a
wide range of clubs across Britain. He chose Celtic and
the transfer became the most expensive between two
Scottish clubs. Tony Mowbray named him as the new club
captain after Stephen McManus' exit in January 2010 and
the midfielder has proved to be an inspirational leader. He
had to undergo surgery last season, which ruled him out
for three months, but on his return, the Hoops enjoyed a
magnificent winning run with Brown in the driving seat of
their success.

CELTIC FC

No.15 KRIS COMMONS
POSITION: Attacking Midfielder
DATE OF BIRTH: 30/08/83
BORN: Nottingham, England
HEIGHT: 5'6"

PREVIOUS CLUBS:
Stoke City, Nottingham Forest, Derby County

CELTIC DEBUT: *v Aberdeen (n) 4-1,*
League Cup, 29/01/11

APPEARANCES:	GOALS:
League: 27 + 11 sub	*League: 12*
League Cup: 2 + 2 sub	*League Cup: 1*
Scottish Cup: 17 + 1 sub	*Scottish Cup: 2*
Europe: 1 + 3 sub	*TOTAL: 15*
TOTAL: 37 + 17 sub	

Celtic won the battle to sign Commons in January 2011, but after playing his football for more than a decade south of the border, some fans may have been unaware of what to expect from the player they had only really seen representing Scotland on the odd occasion. What they saw after his arrival, however, more than impressed them. He burst on to the scene, scoring six minutes into his debut, and then again the following week against Rangers. He became an instant hero with the Celtic support but injuries last season made it difficult for him to replicate that form. He made a comeback towards the end of the campaign, however, and saved his only goal of the season for a special strike against Rangers.

CELTIC FC

No.16 JOE LEDLEY
POSITION: Midfielder
DATE OF BIRTH: 12/07/87
BORN: Cardiff, Wales
HEIGHT: 6'0"

PREVIOUS CLUBS:
Cardiff City

CELTIC DEBUT: *v SC Braga (a) 0-3,*
UEFA Champions League qualifier, 28/07/10

APPEARANCES:	GOALS:
League: 57 + 4 sub	*League: 9*
League Cup: 8	*League Cup: 1*
Scottish Cup: 8	*Scottish Cup: 4*
Europe: 10 + 1 sub	*Europe: 1*
TOTAL: 83 + 4 sub	*Total: 15*

Having played for his boyhood heroes, Cardiff City, all his life, the move to Celtic in the summer of 2010 was a new and exciting challenge for Ledley. But he has grabbed the opportunity with both hands and shown since his arrival he is more than capable of becoming a long-serving Celtic favourite. The Welshman has been one of the Hoops' most consistent and versatile players in recent years, filling in at left-back and left-midfield almost as much as his more preferred central midfield position. He has also been a goal threat as well, with his most significant being the winner against Rangers three days after Christmas in the 2011/12 season.

CELTIC FC

No.18 KI SUNG YUENG
POSITION: Midfielder
DATE OF BIRTH: 24/01/89
BORN: South Korea
HEIGHT: 6'2"

PREVIOUS CLUBS:
FC Seoul

CELTIC DEBUT: *v Falkirk (h) 1-1,*
Scottish Premier League, 16/01/10

APPEARANCES:
League: 44 + 22 sub
League Cup: 3 + 3 sub
Scottish Cup: 6
Europe: 8 + 1 sub
TOTAL: 61 + 26 sub

GOALS:
League: 9
Scottish Cup: 1
Europe: 1
TOTAL: 11

South Korean internationalist, Ki, lived in Australia for four years where he attended college, developed his football skills and learned to speak fluent English. On his return home he joined FC Seoul and soon after became a regular in the national team. It took a while for Ki to adapt to the Scottish game after signing for Celtic in January 2011 but has since become a vital part of the squad. The midfielder has delightful skills, a good reading of the game and specialises in long-range drives from outside of the box. He has also done well to not let the regular long journeys back to Asia for international matches affect his football at Celtic.

CELTIC FC

No.20 PADDY McCOURT
POSITION: Winger
DATE OF BIRTH: 16/12/83
BORN: Derry, Ireland
HEIGHT: 5'11"

PREVIOUS CLUBS:
Rochdale, Shamrock Rovers, Derry City

CELTIC DEBUT: *v Hibernian (h) 4-2,*
Scottish Premier League, 25/10/08

APPEARANCES:	GOALS:
League: 11 + 39 sub	*League: 9*
League Cup: 1 + 4 sub	*League Cup: 1*
Scottish Cup: 2 + 5 sub	*TOTAL: 10*
Europe: 2 + 4 sub	
TOTAL: 16 + 52 sub	

Paddy McCourt has emerged as a cult hero among the Celtic fans in recent years for his incredible skill and ball control. He enjoyed the early years of his career at Shamrock Rovers and Derry City after graduating from Rochdale's youth system. The Irishman has found it difficult to get into Celtic's starting XI over the years, but has made many substitute appearances. Despite the majority of his appearances coming from the bench, he has remained a fans' favourite and his name is regularly sung during the games.

CELTIC FC

No.33 BERAM KAYAL
POSITION: Midfielder
DATE OF BIRTH: 02/05/88
BORN: Jadeidi, Israel
HEIGHT: 5'10"

PREVIOUS CLUBS:
Maccabi Haifa

CELTIC DEBUT: *v FC Utrecht (h) 2-0,*
UEFA Europa League qualifier, 19/08/10

APPEARANCES:	GOALS:
League: 36 + 4 sub	*League: 2*
League Cup: 4	*TOTAL: 2*
Scottish Cup: 5	
Europe: 9	
TOTAL: 54 + 4 sub	

Kayal arrived in the summer of 2010 at the age of 22 as a largely unknown quantity in this country. He had played his football at his boyhood heroes, Maccabi Haifa, since he was 14, and enjoyed four years in their senior side. Upon moving to Scotland, however, he made an immediate impact and became a fans' favourite inside his first season. He continued his form into the 2011/12 campaign and was an influential figure in European matches when he played in the defensive midfield position. An ankle injury sustained against Rangers in December, however, ruled him out for five months but he made his long-awaited comeback in the final game of the season, much to the delight of the crowd.

CELTIC FC

No.40 RABIU IBRAHIM

POSITION: Midfielder
DATE OF BIRTH: 15/03/91
BORN: Kano, Nigeria
HEIGHT: 5'7"

PREVIOUS CLUBS:
Gateway, Sporting CP, Real Massama,
PSV Eindhoven

CELTIC DEBUT: *v St Johnstone (h) 1-0,*
Scottish Premier League, 03/05/12

APPEARANCES:
League: 1 sub
TOTAL: 1 sub

Ibrahim signed a three-and-half-year contract with the Hoops in January 2012 after ending his contract with Dutch side PSV Eindhoven the previous month. The Nigerian attacking midfielder started his professional career in Europe in 2007 with Sporting Lisbon and spent some time on loan with Real Sport Clube in Portugal's third division. While on loan in 2009, he rejected Sporting's offer of a professional contract and even then there was talk of the player coming to Celtic. He finally got the move he wanted when his work permit was granted on January 23, 2012 and he made his debut four months later.

CELTIC FC

No.46 DYLAN McGEOUCH
POSITION: Midfielder
DATE OF BIRTH: 15/01/93
BORN: Glasgow
HEIGHT: 5'10"

PREVIOUS CLUBS:
Celtic, Rangers

CELTIC DEBUT: *v Motherwell (a) 2-1,*
Scottish Premier League, 06/11/11

APPEARANCES: **GOALS:**
League: 1 + 5 sub   *League: 1*
Scottish Cup: 2 sub   *TOTAL: 1*
TOTAL: 1 + 7 sub

McGeouch grabbed the headlines when he signed a
pre-contract with Celtic in December 2010, rejoining the
club from Rangers. As well as featuring for the Under-19
side, McGeouch was pushed into the Development Squad
on his return and was in and around the first-team more
and more towards the end of the campaign. It was his
stunning strike, at the end of a 70-yard run, against
St Mirren that catapulted him into the limelight on his
home debut in November 2011.

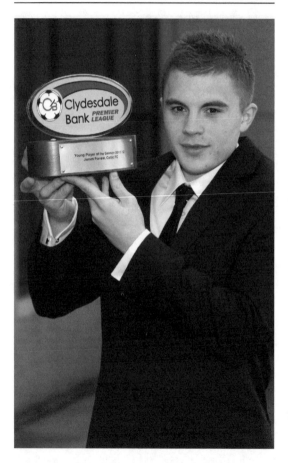

CELTIC FC

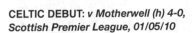

No.46 JAMES FORREST
POSITION: Midfielder
DATE OF BIRTH: 07/07/91
BORN: Prestwick, Scotland
HEIGHT: 5'8"

CELTIC DEBUT: *v Motherwell (h) 4-0,*
Scottish Premier League, 01/05/10

APPEARANCES: GOALS:
League: 38 + 12 sub   *League: 11*
League Cup: 4   *League Cup: 3*
Scottish Cup: 2 + 3 sub   *Total: 13*
Europe: 7 + 3 sub
TOTAL: 51 + 18 sub

The Youth Academy graduate has progressed with every
season he has been in the first-team. He made his scoring
debut towards the end of the 2009/10 season after being
included in many squads before that. But it was his
outstanding performances in the 2011/12 campaign which
made him one of the star players in the squad and as a
result, the winger lifted every Young Player of the Year award
up for grabs. He has shown maturity on the pitch beyond his
age and is an inspiration to the other young players at the
club. As well as being able to play on either flank, he also
provides a new option in European matches by playing just
behind the strikers.

CELTIC FC

No.56 FILIP TWARDZIK
POSITION: Midfielder
DATE OF BIRTH: 10/02/93
BORN: Trinec, Czech Republic
HEIGHT: 6'2"

CELTIC DEBUT: *v Peterhead (a) 3-0, Scottish Cup, 08/01/12*

APPEARANCES:
League: 1 sub
Scottish Cup: 2 sub
TOTAL: 3 sub

The midfielder moved to Scotland with his twin brother, Patrik, who has also worked his way through the youth set-up to reach the Development Squad. Filip has been in the manager's plans for a long time now and played against Lyon in the Emirates Cup in July 2010. He made his competitive first-team debut in January 2012, against Peterhead in the Scottish Cup, and came on as a substitute again in the next round. The versatile player, who can attack just as well as he can defend, also has six medals from his three years in the Hoops' Under-19 side.

CELTIC FC

No.67 VICTOR WANYAMA
POSITION: Midfielder
DATE OF BIRTH: 25/06/91
BORN: Nairobi, Kenya
HEIGHT: 6'2"

PREVIOUS CLUBS:
JMJ Youth Academy, Nairobi City Stars,
AFC Leopards, Helsingborgs, Beershot AC

CELTIC DEBUT: v St Johnstone (h) 0-1,
Scottish Premier League, 21/08/11

APPEARANCES:	GOALS:
League: 24 + 5 sub	*League: 4*
League Cup: 2 + 2 sub	*TOTAL: 4*
Scottish Cup: 2 + 2 sub	
Europe: 5	
TOTAL: 33 + 9 sub	

While some players may suffer a culture shock when they move to Scotland, the Kenyan midfielder settled almost instantly. He had a head start having learned his trade in Sweden, at youth level, before moving to Belgium, and he adapted to the Scottish game in no time at all. His physical strength belies his youth and he has a long, bright future ahead of him. He was impressive in both central-midfield and defence last season and scored a screamer of a goal to win the game against Hearts in December. If it hadn't been for James Forrest's outstanding contribution, Wanyama would have been a strong candidate for the Young Player of the Year awards last season.

CELTIC FC

No.30 PAUL SLANE
POSITION: Midfielder
DATE OF BIRTH: 25/11/91
BORN: Glasgow
HEIGHT: 5'10"

PREVIOUS CLUBS:
Motherwell, MK Dons (loan)

CELTIC DEBUT: *n/a*

Arrived from Motherwell in January 2010, on the same day as Robbie Keane, who came on loan from Spurs. Since then the young midfielder has suffered a string of unlucky injuries. He started a pre-season friendly in Lincoln in 2010 but exited after a cruciate knee ligament injury. That kept him out for the rest of the season but the following year, he was named on the bench for the UEFA Europa League qualifier against FC Sion. He spent the second-half of the campaign on loan at MK Dons.

CELTIC FC

No.50 PAUL GEORGE
POSITION: Winger
DATE OF BIRTH: 27/01/94
BORN: Killough, Ireland
HEIGHT: 5'8"

CELTIC DEBUT: *v Ross County (a) 2-0,*
League Cup, 21/11/11

APPEARANCES:
League Cup: 1 sub
TOTAL: 1 sub

Joined Celtic full-time when he was 14-years-old and made his first-team debut, two years later, in April 2010 in a friendly against AZ Alkmaar. He was earmarked at a young age as the one to watch and the Irish midfielder continued to impress when he scored the winning goal against Rangers in the Glasgow Cup final in May 2011. Neil Lennon has never hidden his interest in the creative teenager, who can play up front or on the wing, and handed him his competitive debut against Ross County in September 2011. Unfortunately, a horrific double leg break against Rangers at the end of the 2011/12 season ruled him out of action until Christmas, halting his chances of pushing into the first-team.

CELTIC FC

No.9 GEORGIOS SAMARAS
POSITION: Winger/Striker
DATE OF BIRTH: 21/02/85
BORN: Heraklion, Greece
HEIGHT: 6'4"

PREVIOUS CLUBS:
Manchester City, Heerenveen, OFI Crete

CELTIC DEBUT: *v Kilmarnock (a) 5-1,*
Scottish Cup, 02/02/08

APPEARANCES:	GOALS:
League: 80 + 46 sub	*League: 37*
League Cup: 4 + 4 sub	*League Cup: 5*
Scottish Cup: 11 + 8 sub	*Scottish Cup: 3*
Europe: 21 + 6 sub	*Europe: 4*
TOTAL: 116 + 64 sub	*Total: 49*

Samaras impressed so much during his loan spell at Celtic
in the second half of the 2007/08 season, he was signed up
on a permanent contract. Now as one of the longest-serving
players in the squad, he got to lift his second SPL trophy at
the end of last season. It was a fitting way to end arguably
his best campaign at the club where he was an influential
part of the side. Despite still being a threat on the goals
front, Samaras made an even bigger contribution on the
left wing, providing many goalscoring opportunities for his
team-mates.

CELTIC FC

No.10 ANTHONY STOKES
POSITION: Striker
DATE OF BIRTH: 25/07/88
BORN: Dublin, Ireland
HEIGHT: 5'11"

PREVIOUS CLUBS:
*Hibernian, Crystal Palace (loan), Sheffield United
(loan), Sunderland, Falkirk (loan), Arsenal, Shelbourne*

CELTIC DEBUT: *v Hearts (h) 3-0,*
Scottish Premier League, 11/09/10

APPEARANCES:	GOALS:
League: 47 + 16 sub	*League: 26*
League Cup: 7	*League Cup: 8*
Scottish Cup: 3 + 4 sub	*Scottish Cup: 4*
Europe: 4 + 1 sub	*Europe: 2*
TOTAL: 61 + 21 sub	*TOTAL: 40*

Stokes first made a name for himself in the SPL when he
moved to Falkirk on loan from Arsenal in 2006. He impressed
further for Hibernian, three years later, and after much
speculation he signed for Celtic on the final day of the
transfer window in the summer of 2010. The Irish striker has
been invaluable for the Hoops over the past two seasons and
admitted joining his boyhood heroes was a dream come true.
Stokes battles it out with his strike-partner, Gary Hooper, for
the title of top goal-scorer and despite narrowly losing both
seasons he is also responsible for many assists.

CELTIC FC

No.14 MOHAMED BANGURA
POSITION: Striker
DATE OF BIRTH: 27/07/89
BORN: Kambia, Sierra Leone
HEIGHT: 5'10"

PREVIOUS CLUBS:
Kallon, Varnamo, AIK

CELTIC DEBUT: *v Motherwell (h) 4-0,*
Scottish Premier League, 10/09/11

APPEARANCES:
League: 2+ 6 sub
League Cup: 1 sub
Europe: 1 + 2 sub
TOTAL: 3 + 9 sub

Before Celtic, Sierra Leone striker, Mo Bangura, plied
his trade in Sweden, on-loan to IFK Varnamo, before a
season at AIK. He signed for Celtic at the same time as
Victor Wanyama last year, but injuries have restricted him
from making the same impact as his African counterpart.
He made his debut in the 4-0 win against Motherwell in
September, but a knee injury three months later led to
him requiring surgery and being ruled out for most of the
remaining months of the season. He received his first cap
in 2010 and went on to win the Sierra Leone Player of the
Year award in 2011.

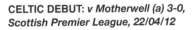

CELTIC FC

No.32 TONY WATT
POSITION: Striker
DATE OF BIRTH: 29/12/93
BORN: Coatbridge
HEIGHT: 6'0"

CELTIC DEBUT: *v Motherwell (a) 3-0,*
Scottish Premier League, 22/04/12

APPEARANCES:	**GOALS:**
League: 3 sub	*League: 2*
TOTAL: 3 sub	*TOTAL: 2*

Watt burst on to the scene in April 2012 when he scored two goals for the first-team, within just six minutes of coming on as a substitute against Motherwell at Fir Park. The Celtic fan had been a scoring revelation since he joined the Hoops' Under-19 set-up from Airdrie United's first-team in January 2011 and was most often utilised as a lone striker. He netted three in the NextGen Series, including two against Barcelona, and struck four inside 35 minutes in an U19 league match against Motherwell. He has also represented Scotland at U19 and U20 level.

CELTIC FC

No.88 GARY HOOPER
POSITION: Striker
DATE OF BIRTH: 26/01/88
BORN: Loughton, England
HEIGHT: 5'9"

PREVIOUS CLUBS:
Scunthorpe United, Hereford United (loan), Leyton Orient (loan), Southend United, Grays Athletic, Maldon Town, Tottenham Hotspur

CELTIC DEBUT: *v SC Braga (h) 2-1, UEFA Champions League qualifier, 04/08/10*

APPEARANCES:
League: 60 + 2 sub
League Cup: 8
Scottish Cup: 8
Europe: 5 + 2 sub
TOTAL: 81 + 4 sub

GOALS:
League: 44
League Cup: 3
Scottish Cup: 1
Europe: 3
TOTAL: 51

The striker started his football career in Spurs' youth academy but when it came to his senior playing days, he started off lower down the divisions. Working his way up from non-league side, Grays Athletic, he gradually moved up through the ranks before winning a move to Celtic in 2010. Since then he has been the Hoops' main striker and has won a wealth of personal awards in just two seasons. He finished the club's top scorer at the end of both campaigns, won the Golden Boot for the SPL in 2011/12 and was named in the SPFA SPL Team of the Year two years in a row.

CELTIC FC

No.28 JAMES KEATINGS
POSITION: Striker
DATE OF BIRTH: 20/01/92
BORN: Glasgow, Scotland
HEIGHT: 5'7"

PREVIOUS CLUBS:
St Johnstone (loan)

CELTIC DEBUT: *n/a*

Despite missing half the 2010/11 Under-19 season through injury, Keatings still finished the campaign as the league's top scorer on 21 goals. He has been a regular in the Scotland national side's youth set-up since he was a schoolboy, showing similar scoring prowess for his country. The striker, who has also played in midfield during his time at Celtic, suffered a cruciate knee ligament injury at the end of last season but agreed to a new deal which would keep him at the club beyond his recovery. Keatings has been on the brink of breaking into the first-team since graduating from the U19s, but took up the option of a loan move to St Johnstone for the second half of the 2011/12 season.

SEASON 2011/12 REVIEW

JULY

Australia was the destination for Celtic's opening pre-season trip and the supporters turned out in droves to welcome the side and gave the new Bhoys a hint of what to expect at the club. Among the new intake were Adam Matthews and Kelvin Wilson while Victor Wanyama completed his transfer and was ready to meet up with his new team-mates when they returned from Down Under. The Hoops lost 1-0 to Central Coast Mariners but recorded wins over Perth Glory (2-0) and Melbourne Victory (1-0). Other friendlies included a 1-0 away win over Cardiff City and a 2-0 home defeat to Wolves before a trip across the Irish Sea saw a 2-0 loss to Inter Milan followed by a 5-0 win over an Airtricity League of Ireland Select in the Dublin Cup. However, in among all that, the real stuff started when Celtic travelled to Easter Road to kick-off the league campaign and returned with all three points thanks to goals from Anthony Stokes and Ki Sung Yueng in a 2-0 win. Through the out door went Graham Carey who joined St Mirren and Morten Rasmussen who moved to Turkish side Sivasspor on loan.

AUGUST

A return trip to Wales beckoned at the start of the month as Swansea City beat the Celts 2-0 but back on the competitive scene, the Hoops returned to SPL action with another away win, this time 1-0 over Aberdeen at Pittodrie with Anthony Stokes again finding the net. However, the win came at a cost when it was revealed that an injury to the previous season's Player of the Year, Emilio Izaguirre, was a fractured ankle that was scheduled to keep him out for up to six months. Dundee United were the first SPL visitors to Celtic Park and five Hoops shared the scoring duties as they romped to a 5-1 win over the Tannadice side. Next up was Europa League play-off duty and FC Sion were the first continental visitors to Celtic Park and the fact that they weren't the last was down to their brazen disregard of the rules and lack of integrity off the pitch rather than any incompetence on it. To cut a long story short, they flouted a transfer ban and also washed their dirty linen in a civil court resulting in UEFA awarding two 3-0 wins to Celtic after a 0-0 draw and a 3-1 defeat. The Celts also suffered a rare 1-0 home defeat to St Johnstone before ending the month on a high with a 2-0 away win over St Mirren courtesy of two Gary Hooper goals. Player movement continued with Fraser Forster again joining on loan from Newcastle United. Going in the opposite direction were Shaun Maloney who moved to Wigan and Jos Hooiveld who joined Southampton while Ritchie Towell and Daryl Murphy went on loan to Hibs and Ipswich Town respectively.

Gary Hooper during
pre-season training
in Australia

SEPTEMBER

Once the summer transfer window was closed and the friendlies were
out of the road, Neil Lennon and the team could concentrate on the
fixture schedule, although the Sion debacle hadn't been fully resolved at
that point. On the football front, the month kicked off with a 4-0 home
win over Motherwell before the Celts flew out on Europa League duty
to Spain to take on Atletico Madrid. The Spanish side won 2-0 and Ibrox
was next on the cards and, despite leading 2-1 at half-time, the Celts lost
4-2 in the first derby of the season. The first League Cup tie of the term
featured a trip to play Ross County and a 2-0 win over the Highland side
was followed by another northern team, Inverness CT, making the trip to
Celtic Park where another 2-0 win for the Hoops was the outcome. Italian
side Udinese were the next to come calling and a heartbreaking penalty
equaliser two minutes from the end cancelled out a Ki spot-kick at the
start of the match.

OCTOBER

The month of October was to be a defining one for Neil Lennon's Celts
and it started with a 2-0 defeat at Tynecastle and things seemed to go
from bad to worse in the next game as Kilmarnock took a 3-0 lead into
the Rugby Park dressing room at half-time. We can only guess what the
manager said during the break – but it had the desired effect as three
goals in a seven-minute spell pulled not only the game but, ultimately, the
season around. That may not have been evident at the time but a 1-1 away
draw with Rennes followed up by a 2-0 home win over Aberdeen preceded
a double-header against Hibs. The League Cup tie was won 4-1 at Easter
Road before the SPL match at Celtic Park was drawn 0-0 – this would be
the last match in which Celtic would drop points at home.

NOVEMBER

A 3-1 home win over Rennes opened Celtic's account for the month but
the big news was that, going into a match against Motherwell at Fir Park,
Celtic were 15 points behind Rangers and three behind the Lanarkshire
club – people were already making stark claims that the league was over.
Celtic came from behind to win 2-1 at Fir Park and the quiet chipping away
continued. Further wins over Inverness CT, Dunfermline and St Mirren
followed and the only perceived blip in an otherwise textbook month was
the final 1-0 defeat to eventual trophy winners, Atletico Madrid in the
Europa League. The month finished with Celtic and Rangers both having
played 16 games – and that 15-point lead had shrunk somewhat to only
four points.

DECEMBER

A close 1-1 draw in Udinese ended Celtic's interest in the Europa League but all eyes were on the SPL situation prior to that game with the Hoops recording two tight 1-0 wins over Dundee United and Hearts with the home game against the Edinburgh side proving particularly pivotal. It was against Hearts that a wonder goal from Victor Wanyama and a last-minute penalty save by Fraser Forster kept Celtic in the title hunt at a crucial point in the season. Celtic followed that up with a 2-0 win over St Johnstone at McDiarmid Park and, all the while, Rangers had been matching Celtic by also recording three wins in their first three SPL games of December. Then, on Christmas Eve, Celtic fans everywhere had an early present opened up for them as the Hoops' 2-1 home win over Kilmarnock came on the same day as Rangers going down 2-1 to St Mirren in Paisley. Celtic were now one point behind and, four days later, would play Rangers at Celtic Park – the place just about erupted when Joe Ledley headed in a 52nd-minute header to put Celtic at the top of the league by two points – it was a lead that would only increase as the season wore on.

JANUARY

There were five straight wins recorded in the first month of the New Year, three in the SPL and one each in the Scottish Cup and League Cup, and Celtic started off by first-footing Dunfermline and recording a 3-0 win. That result was repeated the following week in another away game, this time in the Scottish Cup and it was Highland side Peterhead who were on the receiving end. The winning run continued with full points earned against Dundee United in a 2-1 win at home and St Mirren in a 2-0 away win. The month was wrapped up with a 3-1 win over Falkirk in the semi-final of the League Cup. Celtic's lead at the top of the table had increased to seven points by the end of the month. There was also some more movement in the transfer market with Polish striker Pawel Brozek arriving on loan from Trabzonspor in Turkey and Rabiu Ibrahim arriving from PSV Eindhoven. Four Celts moved out on loan with Lewis Toshney going to Kilmarnock, Josh Thompson to Chesterfield, Paul Slane to MK Dons and James Keatings to St Johnstone.

FEBRUARY

Not only did Celtic record six straight wins in February, they did that without conceding a single goal. Indeed, by the end of the month, Celtic had gone 17 games unbeaten (the last team to beat them was Atletico Madrid in November) and 24 domestic games unbeaten (the last team to beat them was Hearts in October).The month began with a 2-0 Scottish Cup win in

Inverness followed by a resounding 4-0 victory over Hearts at Tynecastle. Inverness cropped up again in the league, this time at home, and a 1-0 win was added to the tally before another rewarding trip to the capital delivered a 5-0 win over Hibs. Then came two home games in quick succession with Dunfermline losing 2-0 and Motherwell 1-0. Celtic's lead at the end of the month would have increased to 10 points but Rangers' deduction for going into administration on St Valentine's Day saw that stretch to 20 points.

MARCH

Celtic Park was an empty fortress during the month of March as the card showed three away matches and a trip to Hampden for the League Cup final against Kilmarnock. The month opened with a bumpy trip to Pittodrie where a cruel deflected own-goal ensured that a 1-1 draw ended that six-game run of consecutive clean sheets as well as Celtic's 20-game domestic winning run. Another trip north followed with a Scottish Cup 4-0 victory over Dundee United but Celtic fell to their first domestic defeat after 26 games in the next game – and, unfortunately, that was a 1-0 loss to Kilmarnock against the run of play in the League Cup final. Despite that 1-1 draw with Aberdeen, Celtic's lead had increased to 21 points throughout the month and that's the way it stayed until the final game and a trip to Ibrox. The Celts received two red cards but, in the end, were unlucky to lose 3-2 and the lead sat at 18 points.

The superb Celtic following at Carrow Road

APRIL

The penultimate month of the football calendar was one in which the obvious highs far outweighed the one low of losing out in the Scottish Cup semi-final 2-1 to Hearts by an extra-time penalty that should never have been. The first high was within touching distance following Celtic's 2-0 win over St Johnstone in the opening game of the month. Those three points meant that the title could be clinched in the following match when the Hoops visited Kilmarnock. Any win would do but Neil Lennon wanted his charges to do it in style at a Rugby Park heaving on three sides with Celtic supporters. Celtic's season turned around six months earlier when both sides shared six goals in a 3-3 draw. The same tally of goals would be scored in this game but they were all for Celtic as the Hoops tore the home side apart. Motherwell were the next SPL opponents and a 3-0 win was recorded at Fir Park with debutant teenager Tony Watt scoring twice. That left the last derby meeting and a rampant Celtic side swept Rangers' challenge aside with a 3-0 win. Celtic finished the month 21 points ahead of their rivals.

MAY

Amazingly, after winning the title in the week before the SPL split, Celtic had to wait until the last game of the season before being presented with the trophy – and at the start of May, that was still three games away. St Johnstone were first up and a 1-0 win at home delivered another three points in a midweek match but there was a slip just three days later when a lacklustre performance at Tannadice resulted in a 1-0 defeat. That left the final game and the presentation of the gleaming SPL trophy. Hearts were the visitors at a packed Celtic Park and Neil Lennon demanded that the team repay the supporters by delivering the silverware in style. And, once more, the players responded magnificently by totally overpowering the visitors with Gary Hooper leading the line in top form by scoring all FIVE of Celtic's goals in the 5-0 win. On any other day the striker would have at least equalled Dixie Deans' post-war record of six goals in one game and Jimmy McGrory's all-time record of eight goals in one game would have been under threat. That just paved the way for the glorious title celebrations that followed and, somewhat fittingly, it was the supporters who took the plaudits as the curtain came down on a memorable season. The reason? It was a testimonial for Adam Drury of Norwich and, despite a young Celtic side losing 2-0, it was the Hoops support who stole the show in earning more plaudits from far and wide after their performance before, during and after the 90 minutes at Carrow Road.

A CHAMPION
VIEW

**Subscribe to Celtic Football Club
Weekly Magazine for the 2012/13 season**

CELTIC'S
HISTORY

AND IF YOU KNOW THE HISTORY...

NOVEMBER 6, 1887
Celtic Football Club is formally constituted in St Mary's Church Hall in East Rose Street (now Forbes Street), Calton. The purpose is stated as being to alleviate poverty in Glasgow's East End parishes.

MAY 28, 1888
Celtic beat Rangers 5-2 in a 'friendly'. It is the new club's first match and is played on the first Celtic Park.

1889
Celtic reach the final of the Scottish Cup in their first full season of competition, but they lose 2-1 to the well-established Third Lanark. However, the club wins its first trophy, the North-Eastern Cup (a local competition), beating Cowlairs 6-1 in the final.

1892
Celtic win the Scottish Cup for the first time in their history by defeating Queen's Park 5-1 in the final at Ibrox. A few months later, the club moves to its present ground.

1893
Celtic win their first Scottish League Championship.

1897
The club becomes a private limited liability company and Willie Maley is appointed secretary-manager.

1905-1910
Celtic win the League Championship for six successive seasons.

1907
Celtic achieve the 'Double' by winning the Scottish Cup and the League Championship in the same season, the first time the feat has been achieved in the history of the national sport. The team

repeats the achievement the following season.

1914-1917
Celtic win the championship four times in a row.

1925
Celtic beat Dundee 2-1 to win the Scottish Cup, with Patsy Gallacher scoring his famous 'somersault' goal, leaping over defenders and into the Dundee net with the ball between his feet.

1931
Goalkeeper John Thomson dies as a result of head injuries suffered during a match against Rangers on September 5.

1937
Celtic beat Aberdeen in a Scottish Cup final, watched by a record crowd of 146,433 at Hampden Park. The attendance remains a record for a club match in Europe.

1939
Celtic win the Empire Exhibition Trophy by defeating Everton 1-0 at Ibrox after extra time in the final.

1940
Jimmy McStay takes over as Celtic manager following the retirement of Willie Maley.

1945
Former player and ex-captain Jimmy McGrory replaces Jimmy McStay as manager.

1953
Celtic defeat Hibernian 2-0 in the final of the Coronation Cup, held to celebrate the crowning of Queen Elizabeth II. The invited teams included the best in Scotland and England, and the final attracts a crowd of 117,000 at Hampden Park.

1954
A League and Scottish Cup Double is secured with a 2-1 victory over Aberdeen in the final at Hampden.

1956
Celtic win the League Cup for the first time in their history by beating Partick Thistle 3-0 in a replay.

1957
Celtic retain the League Cup in memorable style by thrashing Rangers 7-1 in the final. Billy McPhail scores a hat-trick, while there were also goals for Neilly Mochan (2), Sammy Wilson, and Willie Fernie.

1965
Jock Stein succeeds Jimmy McGrory as manager in March 1965, and guides the team to the first victory in a Scottish Cup final in 11 years. Billy McNeill's dramatic header seals a 3-2 win over Dunfermline Athletic.

1966
Celtic win the championship for the first time in 12 seasons, and reach the semi-final of the Cup-Winners' Cup again before losing 2-1 on aggregate to Liverpool.

1967
Celtic complete their most glorious season by winning every competition entered: Scottish League, Scottish Cup, League Cup, Glasgow Cup and the European Cup. The climax of the season is the 2-1 victory over Inter Milan in the European Cup final played at the Estadio Nacional in Lisbon, May 25, 1967. Celtic became the first British (and non-Latin) club to win Europe's most coveted trophy.

1970
Celtic reach the final of the European Cup again, but lose 2-1 to Feyenoord after extra time in Milan. In the semi-final

Celtic defeated Leeds United in both legs. The second leg at Hampden Park was watched by 133,961, the largest crowd ever to watch a match in European club competition.

1974
Celtic win the league championship for the ninth season in a row - at the time, a joint world record for success in domestic titles.

1977
Celtic win the Double – Jock Stein's last major honours as Celtic manager – with Kenny Dalglish, Pat Stanton and Danny McGrain the three key players for the Hoops.

1978
Billy McNeill, captain of the 1967 team, succeeds Jock Stein as manager. During Stein's 12-year tenure (excluding 1975/76, when he was recuperating from injuries received in a car accident), the club enjoyed 25 successes in major competitions: the European Cup, 10 Championships, 8 Scottish Cups and 6 League Cups.

1979
Billy McNeill guides Celtic to the league championship in his first season as manager. The title is gained in truly dramatic fashion at Celtic Park with a 4-2 win over neighbours Rangers in the club's final match. It becomes known as the night '10-men-won-the-league', after Johnny Doyle is red-carded early in the match.

1983
Another ex-player, David Hay, replaces Billy McNeill as manager.

1985
Celtic win the Scottish Cup by beating Dundee United 2-1 at Hampden Park in the 100th cup final.

1986

Celtic snatch the championship by edging out Hearts on the last day of the campaign. The margin is on goal difference, as Celtic beat St Mirren 5-0 at Love Street and Hearts lose 2-0 at Dens Park.

1987

Billy McNeill returns to Celtic Park as manager, replacing David Hay.

1988

Celtic celebrate the centenary season (1987/88) by winning the first Double in 11 years. The accomplishment marks the 35th league title, and the 28th Scottish Cup.

1989

Celtic win the Scottish Cup for the 29th time as Joe Miller's goal sinks Rangers by 1-0.

1991

Liam Brady becomes Celtic's manager when he takes over from Billy McNeill. His appointment marks a break from tradition, as he is the first Celtic manager never to have played for the club.

1993

Liam Brady is replaced as manager by former-Celt Lou Macari.

1994

In March, Fergus McCann rescues the club from financial ruin. Shortly afterwards, Lou Macari is replaced as manager by Tommy Burns. Later that same year, the club is reconstituted as a plc, a development quickly followed by the most successful share-issue in the history of British football.

1995

Celtic play home fixtures at Hampden Park during season 1994/95, while Celtic Park is undergoing the first phase of a reconstruction. The 'exile' ends with a 1-0 victory over Airdrie in the Scottish Cup

final, marking the club's 30th triumph in the competition and also the first major trophy since 1989.

1997

Tommy Burns is replaced by the Dutch coach Wim Jansen, ironically a member of the Feyenoord side which defeated Celtic in the European Cup final in Milan in 1970. In 1997 he guides Celtic to the first League Cup final victory in 15 years in a 3-0 defeat of Dundee United at Ibrox Park.

1998

Celtic 'stop the 10', winning their first league title in a decade and preventing Rangers from making it 10-in-a-row. However, Wim Jansen departs almost immediately and is replaced for the start of the new campaign by Dr Jozef Venglos.

1999

In April, Fergus McCann departs at the completion of his five-year stint. Allan MacDonald, a former British Aerospace managing director, succeeds him as chief executive. A few months later Dr Venglos retires and is replaced by John Barnes, with Kenny Dalglish installed as director of football operations.

2000

A shock 3-1 defeat at Celtic Park in the Scottish Cup by Inverness Caledonian Thistle in February leads to the departure of John Barnes, with Kenny Dalglish taking control of team matters until the end of the season. He steers Celtic to victory in the League Cup final. During the summer Martin O'Neill takes over as Celtic's manager and he endears himself to the support by masterminding an astonishing 6-2 league victory over Rangers at Celtic Park on August 27.

2001

A treble-winning season for the Hoops. They beat Kilmarnock 3-0 in the League

Cup final and beat Hibernian by the same scoreline in the Scottish Cup final. And a Tommy Johnson goal beats St Mirren at Celtic Park to seal the title. The season also sees Henrik Larsson score 53 goals, including 35 league goals, to win Europe's Golden Boot Award. The following season, Celtic compete in the UEFA Champions League group stages for the first time.

2003

Celtic reach the UEFA Cup final – their first European final in 33 years. Over 80,000 fans flock to Seville, but see the Hoops lose 3-2 in extra-time to FC Porto of Portugal. Days later, they miss out on the SPL title by a single goal.

2004

Celtic win the league title convincingly, while Henrik Larsson leaves the club after seven magnificent years, scoring 242 goals in 315 appearances – becoming the third top goalscorer in the club's history.

2005

Heartache on the final day of the league season as Celtic lose 2-0 at Fir Park to miss out on the title in Martin O'Neill's last season. The Hoops win the Scottish Cup a week later with a 1-0 win over Dundee United. Gordon Strachan takes over as Celtic manager.

2006

Celtic win the League Cup with a victory over Dunfermline just days after Jimmy Johnstone, the Greatest Ever Celt, dies, and they also win the SPL title. It means automatic qualification into the group stages of the UEFA Champions League, and a 1-0 victory over Manchester United courtesy of a Shunsuke Nakamura goal and an Artur Boruc penalty save, means the club qualifies for the knockout stages for the first time.

2007

Celtic retain the league title, securing it with a victory over Kilmarnock at Rugby Park. In the UEFA Champions League last 16, they are knocked out by eventual winners AC Milan. The Hoops also secure the Double with a 1-0 win over Dunfermline in Neil Lennon's last game for the club.

2008

Celtic legend, and first-team coach, Tommy Burns, passes away. Days later, a third league title is won at Tannadice on an emotional night, the triumph being dedicated him.

2009

Celtic win the League Cup with a 2-0 extra-time win over Rangers, thanks to goals from Darren O'Dea and Aiden McGeady, but lose out on a fourth league title in a row. Gordon Strachan leaves as Celtic manager and is replaced by Tony Mowbray.

2010

After a mixed few months of the campaign, Tony Mowbray is sacked following a 4-0 defeat against St Mirren. Neil Lennon takes over as interim manager, but can't prevent a disastrous Scottish Cup semi-final exit against Ross County. His team, however, wins all eight of their league matches, and he is appointed full-time manager.

2011

Neil Lennon wins his first trophy as Celtic manager with a 3-0 victory over Motherwell in the Scottish Cup final, having narrowly lost out in the SPL and League Cup final.

2012

Celtic win their 43rd championship after being 15 points behind in November but they were back on top by the end of December and that's where they stayed.

LEAGUE POSITION SEASON BY SEASON

SEASON	P	W	D	L	F	A	GD	PTS	POS
1890/91	18	11	3	4	48	21	27	25	*3
1891/92	22	16	3	3	62	21	41	35	2
1892/93	18	14	1	3	54	25	29	29	1
1893/94	18	14	1	3	53	32	21	29	1
1894/95	18	11	4	3	50	29	21	26	2
1895/96	18	15	0	3	64	25	39	30	1
1896/97	18	10	4	4	42	18	24	24	4
1897/98	18	15	3	0	56	13	43	33	1
1898/99	18	11	2	5	51	33	18	24	3
1899/00	18	9	7	2	46	27	19	25	2
1900/01	20	13	3	4	49	28	21	29	2
1901/02	18	11	4	3	38	28	10	26	2
1902/03	22	8	10	4	36	30	6	26	5
1903/04	26	18	2	6	69	28	41	38	3
1904/05	26	18	5	3	68	31	37	41	1
1905/06	30	24	1	5	76	19	57	49	1
1906/07	34	23	9	2	80	30	50	55	1
1907/08	34	24	7	3	86	27	59	55	1
1908/09	34	23	5	6	71	24	47	51	1
1909/10	34	24	6	4	63	22	41	54	1
1910/11	34	15	11	8	48	18	30	41	5
1911/12	34	17	11	6	58	33	25	45	2
1912/13	34	22	5	7	53	28	25	49	2

SEASON	P	W	D	L	F	A	GD	PTS	POS
1913/14	38	30	5	3	81	14	67	65	1
1914/15	38	30	5	3	91	25	66	65	1
1915/16	38	32	3	3	116	23	93	67	1
1916/17	38	27	10	1	79	17	62	64	1
1917/18	34	24	7	3	66	26	40	55	2
1918/19	34	26	6	2	71	22	49	58	1
1919/20	42	29	10	3	89	31	58	68	2
1920/21	42	30	6	6	86	35	51	66	2
1921/22	42	27	13	2	83	20	63	67	1
1922/23	38	19	8	11	52	39	13	46	3
1923/24	38	17	12	9	56	33	23	46	3
1924/25	38	18	8	12	77	44	33	44	4
1925/26	38	25	8	5	97	40	57	58	1
1926/27	38	21	7	10	101	55	46	49	3
1927/28	38	23	9	6	93	39	54	55	2
1928/29	38	22	7	9	67	44	23	51	2
1929/30	38	22	5	11	88	46	42	49	4
1930/31	38	24	10	4	101	34	67	58	2
1931/32	38	20	8	10	94	50	44	48	3
1932/33	38	20	8	10	75	44	31	48	4
1933/34	38	18	11	9	78	53	25	47	3
1934/35	38	24	4	10	92	45	47	52	2
1935/36	38	32	2	4	115	33	82	66	1
1936/37	38	22	8	8	89	58	31	52	3

SEASON	P	W	D	L	F	A	GD	PTS	POS
1937/38	38	27	7	4	114	42	72	61	1
1938/39	38	20	8	10	99	53	46	48	2
1939/40	5	3	0	2	7	7	0	6	
1940-46	NO LEAGUE DUE TO WORLD WAR 2								
1946/47	30	13	6	11	53	55	-2	32	7
1947/48	30	10	5	15	41	56	-15	25	12
1948/49	30	12	7	11	48	40	8	31	6
1949/50	30	14	7	9	51	50	1	35	5
1950/51	30	12	5	13	48	46	2	29	7
1951/52	30	10	8	12	52	55	-3	28	9
1952/53	30	11	7	12	51	54	-3	29	8
1953/54	30	20	3	7	72	29	43	43	1
1954/55	30	19	8	3	76	37	39	46	2
1955/56	34	16	9	9	55	39	16	41	5
1956/57	34	15	8	11	58	43	15	38	5
1957/58	34	19	8	7	84	47	37	46	3
1958/59	34	14	8	12	70	53	17	36	6
1959/60	34	12	9	13	73	59	14	33	9
1960/61	34	15	9	10	64	46	18	39	4
1961/62	34	19	8	7	81	37	44	46	3
1962/63	34	19	6	9	76	44	32	44	4
1963/64	34	19	9	6	89	34	55	47	3
1964/65	34	16	5	13	76	57	19	37	8
1965/66	34	27	3	4	106	30	76	57	1

SEASON	P	W	D	L	F	A	GD	PTS	POS
1966/67	34	26	6	2	111	33	78	58	1
1967/68	34	30	3	1	106	24	82	63	1
1968/69	34	23	8	3	89	32	57	54	1
1969/70	34	27	3	4	96	33	63	57	1
1970/71	34	25	6	3	89	23	66	56	1
1971/72	34	28	4	2	96	28	68	60	1
1972/73	34	26	5	3	93	28	65	57	1
1973/74	34	23	7	4	82	27	55	53	1
1974/75	34	20	5	9	81	41	40	45	3
1975/76	36	21	6	9	71	42	29	48	2
1976/77	36	23	9	4	79	39	40	55	1
1977/78	36	15	6	15	63	54	9	36	5
1978/79	36	21	6	9	61	37	24	48	2
1979/80	36	18	11	7	61	38	23	47	2
1980/81	36	26	4	6	84	37	47	56	1
1981/82	36	24	7	5	79	33	46	55	2
1982/83	36	25	5	6	90	36	54	55	2
1983/84	36	21	8	7	80	41	39	50	2
1984/85	36	22	8	6	77	30	47	52	2
1985/86	36	20	10	6	67	38	29	50	1
1986/87	44	27	9	8	90	41	49	63	2
1987/88	44	31	10	3	79	23	56	72	1
1988/89	36	21	4	11	66	44	22	46	3
1989/90	36	10	14	12	37	37	0	34	5

SEASON	P	W	D	L	F	A	GD	PTS	POS
1990/91	36	17	7	12	52	38	14	41	3
1991/92	44	26	10	8	88	42	46	62	3
1992/93	44	24	12	8	68	41	27	60	3
1993/94	44	15	20	9	51	38	13	50	5
1994/95	36	11	18	7	39	33	6	51	4
1995/96	36	24	11	1	74	25	49	83	2
1996/97	36	23	6	7	78	32	46	75	2
1997/98	36	22	8	6	64	24	40	74	1
1998/99	36	21	8	7	84	35	49	71	2
1999/00	36	21	6	9	90	38	52	69	2
2000/01	38	31	4	3	90	29	61	97	1
2001/02	38	33	4	1	94	18	76	103	1
2002/03	38	31	4	3	98	26	72	97	2
2003/04	38	31	5	2	105	25	80	98	1
2004/05	38	30	2	6	85	35	50	92	2
2005/06	38	29	5	4	93	37	56	92	1
2006/07	38	26	6	6	65	34	31	84	1
2007/08	38	28	5	5	84	26	58	89	1
2008/09	38	24	10	4	80	33	47	82	2
2009/10	38	25	6	7	75	39	36	81	2
2010/11	38	29	5	4	85	22	63	92	2
2011/12	38	30	3	5	84	21	63	93	1

*Four points deducted season 1890/91

LEAGUE RECORD v ALL OPPONENTS

Team	P	W	D	L	F	A
Abercorn	8	7	0	1	31	10
Aberdeen	264	138	61	65	480	296
Airdrieonians	128	88	22	18	311	118
Albion Rovers	18	14	2	2	56	15
Alloa Athletic	2	2	0	0	4	2
Arbroath	18	16	1	1	56	10
Ayr United	76	59	6	11	211	72
Berwick Rangers	0	0	0	0	0	0
Bo'ness	2	2	0	0	5	1
Brechin City	0	0	0	0	0	0
Clyde	126	94	23	9	360	107
Clydebank 1	14	9	3	2	28	10
Clydebank 2	12	9	2	1	31	7
Cowdenbeath	22	17	3	2	62	15
Cowlairs	2	2	0	0	7	0
Dumbarton	40	31	8	1	113	25
Dundee	219	131	45	43	447	230
Dundee United	176	98	44	34	337	185
Dunfermline Ath	101	75	12	14	258	95
East Fife	28	15	4	9	75	48
East Stirlingshire	4	4	0	0	16	4
Falkirk	153	100	29	24	340	148
Hamilton A	89	68	13	8	222	82
Hearts	287	151	66	70	524	321
Hibernian	277	162	65	50	577	277
Inverness CT	21	15	4	2	41	16
Kilmarnock	207	138	43	26	501	195
Leith Athletic	12	10	0	2	37	14
Livingston	16	15	1	0	48	11
Morton	122	83	26	13	275	98
Motherwell	252	152	54	46	544	270
Partick Thistle	182	120	34	28	423	181
Port Glasgow Ath	16	13	2	1	45	11
Queen of the South	40	17	8	15	86	60
Queen's Park	84	65	7	12	220	75
Raith Rovers	80	50	16	14	178	70
Rangers*	305	101	85	119	402	437
St Bernard's	14	12	1	1	37	14
St Johnstone	106	70	18	18	242	94
St Mirren	225	157	38	30	528	199
Stirling Albion	22	14	3	5	64	23
Third Lanark	116	73	21	22	270	132
Vale of Leven	4	2	1	1	18	7

*Includes play-off game in 1905

Celtic supporters celebrate winning the 2011/12 league championship

FIRST AND LAST - LEAGUE

The first and last league games in the Hoops of four Celtic legends...

JIMMY McGRORY

First
Third Lanark 1-0 Celtic
20/01/23

CELTIC'S greatest striker was 18-years-old when he made his debut but the 25,000 crowd at Cathkin saw little to back up his goal-scoring potential and, after another two league games and one Scottish Cup appearance, he was loaned out to Clydebank. He then proceeded to score in a shock win against Celtic and was recalled in a move that rewrote the history of the club.

Last
Celtic 4-3 Queen's Park
16/10/37

GENTLEMAN Jim went out in the only way suitable for such a player – by scoring a vital goal in a 4-3 win in Paradise. Of his 395 league goals, the final five were scored in the 10 games he played that season and those strikes earned the Celts crucial points – and six months after his final game, the Celts became champions by three points over Hearts.

CHARLIE TULLY

First
Celtic 0-0 Morton
14/08/48

THE Irishman's league bow was, in fact, his full Celtic debut on the opening day of the 1948/49 season and despite the Hoops' 12th place finish the previous season, and that fact that they were playing Morton who finished 14th, there was a massive 60,000 at Celtic Park that day – 10,000 more than the crowd at the Rangers game a fortnight later when Tommy Docherty made his Hoops debut.

Last
Aberdeen 3-1 Celtic
27/09/58

CELTIC'S clown prince played his 216th and last league game for the Hoops in an away trip to Aberdeen for the side's fifth game of the campaign. A 20,000 crowd saw the home side take a 3-0 lead by the 55th minute and it was Tully's fellow Irishman, Bertie Peacock, who pulled back the solitary goal for Celtic. Fighting injury, he made a return for Celtic's opening Scottish Cup game, a 4-0 home win over Albion Rovers, on January 31, but he was freed at the end of the season.

DAVIE HAY

First
Celtic 4-1 Aberdeen
06/03/68

JUST turned 20, Davie Hay made his debut from the bench by replacing Charlie Gallagher as a 28,000 crowd took in the visit of Aberdeen. The youngster took to the field amid seven of the Lions who had triumphed in Lisbon just 10 months earlier and he was eased into a game in which the Celts were 4-0 up after 35 minutes thanks to a hat-trick from Bobby Lennox and a single from Billy McNeill.

Last
Morton 0-0 Celtic
06/05/74

HAY'S last ever Hoops game was just two days after he had helped the Celts to lift the Scottish Cup. It was the last game of the 1973/74 season and, therefore, the very last of Celtic's 306 nine-in-a-row matches. The Celt then left for the World Cup in West Germany and, eventually, Chelsea but he would, of course, return to Celtic as manager in 1983.

MURDO MacLEOD

First
Celtic 1-2 Motherwell
04/11/78

AFTER signing from Dumbarton just two days earlier, Murdo MacLeod took to the field against Motherwell and another former Boghead player, Tom McAdam, put the Hoops ahead in the 12th minute. However, the visitors pulled two goals back in a shock win for the soon-to-be relegated Fir Park side. Celtic never lost at home again that season, though, and MacLeod scored the final goal of the term in the 4-2 game.

Last
Hearts 1-0 Celtic
09/05/87

THIS game, the last of the 1986/87 campaign, was also Davie Hay's last as manager before Billy McNeill returned for his second spell as gaffer in time for the centenary year. And, despite Brian McClair scoring 10 goals in the previous seven games, the Celts fired blanks for only the fourth time that season. MacLeod moved to Borussia Dortmund that close season but returned to the Celtic backroom staff in 1997.

SCOTTISH CHAMPIONS

1890/91	Dumbarton & Rangers
1891/92	Dumbarton
1892/93	Celtic
1893/94	Celtic
1894–95	Hearts
1895/96	Celtic
1896/97	Hearts
1897/98	Celtic
1898/99	Rangers
1899/1900	Rangers
1900/01	Rangers
1901/02	Rangers
1902/03	Hibernian
1903/04	Third Lanark
1904/05	Celtic
1905/06	Celtic
1906/07	Celtic
1907/08	Celtic
1908/09	Celtic
1909/10	Celtic
1910/11	Rangers
1911/12	Rangers
1912/13	Rangers
1913/14	Celtic
1914/15	Celtic
1915/16	Celtic
1916/17	Celtic
1917/18	Rangers
1918/19	Celtic
1919/20	Rangers
1920/21	Rangers
1921/22	Celtic
1922/23	Rangers
1923/24	Rangers
1924/25	Rangers
1925/26	Celtic
1926/27	Rangers
1927/28	Rangers
1928/29	Rangers
1929/30	Rangers
1930/31	Rangers
1931/32	Motherwell
1932/33	Rangers
1933/34	Rangers
1934/35	Rangers
1935/36	Celtic
1936/37	Rangers
1937/38	Celtic
1938/39	Rangers

1939–46 League suspended due to the Second World War.

1946/47	Rangers
1947/48	Hibernian
1948/49	Rangers
1949/50	Rangers
1950/51	Hibernian
1951/52	Hibernian
1952/53	Rangers
1953/54	Celtic
1954/55	Aberdeen
1955/56	Rangers
1956/57	Rangers
1957/58	Hearts
1958/59	Rangers
1959/60	Hearts
1960/61	Rangers
1961/62	Dundee
1962/63	Rangers

1963/64	Rangers	1988/89	Rangers
1964/65	Kilmarnock	1989/90	Rangers
1965/66	Celtic	1990/91	Rangers
1966/67	Celtic	1991/92	Rangers
1967/68	Celtic	1992/93	Rangers
1968/69	Celtic	1993/94	Rangers
1969/70	Celtic	1994/95	Rangers
1970/71	Celtic	1995/96	Rangers
1971/72	Celtic	1996/97	Rangers
1972/73	Celtic	1997/98	Celtic
1973/74	Celtic	1998/99	Rangers
1974/75	Rangers	1999/2000	Rangers
1975/76	Rangers	2000/01	Celtic
1976/77	Celtic	2001/02	Celtic
1977/78	Rangers	2002/03	Rangers
1978/79	Celtic	2003/04	Celtic
1979/80	Aberdeen	2004/05	Rangers
1980/81	Celtic	2005/06	Celtic
1981/82	Celtic	2006/07	Celtic
1982/83	Dundee United	2007/08	Celtic
1983/84	Aberdeen	2008/09	Rangers
1984/85	Aberdeen	2009/10	Rangers
1985/86	Celtic	2010/11	Rangers
1986/87	Rangers	2011/12	Celtic
1987/88	Celtic		

Stiliyan Petrov, Martin O'Neill and Didier Agathe celebrate winning the 2003/04 league championship

SCOTTISH CUP FINAL WINNING TEAMS

1892
CELTIC 5-1 QUEEN'S PARK
(Campbell 2, McMahon 2, og)
Cullen, Reynolds, Doyle, W Maley,
Kelly, Gallacher, McCallum, Brady,
Dowds, McMahon, Campbell

1899
CELTIC 2-0 RANGERS
(McMahon, Hodge)
McArthur, Welford, Storrier, Battles,
Marshall, King, Hodge, Campbell,
Divers, McMahon, Bell

1900
CELTIC 4-3 QUEEN'S PARK
(Divers 2, McMahon, Bell)
McArthur, Storrier, Battles, Russell,
Marshall, Orr, Hodge, Campbell,
Divers, McMahon, Bell

1904
CELTIC 3-2 RANGERS
(Quinn 3)
Adams, McLeod, Orr, Young, Loney,
Hay, Muir, McMenemy, Quinn,
Somers, Hamilton

1907
CELTIC 3-0 HEARTS
(Somers 2, Orr)
Adams, McLeod, Orr, Young, McNair,
Hay, Bennett, McMenemy, Quinn,
Somers, Templeton

1908
CELTIC 5-1 ST MIRREN
(Bennett 2, Quinn, Somers, Hamilton)
Adams, McNair, Weir, Young, Loney,

Hay, Bennett, McMenemy, Quinn,
Somers, Hamilton

1911
CELTIC 2-0 HAMILTON
(Quinn, McAteer)
Adams, McNair, Hay, Young, McAteer,
Dodds, McAtee, McMenemy, Quinn,
Kivlichan, Hamilton

1912
CELTIC 2-0 CLYDE
(McMenemy, Gallacher)
Mulrooney, McNair, Dodds, Young,
Loney, Johnstone, McAtee, Gallacher,
Quinn, McMenemy Brown

1914
CELTIC 4-1 HIBERNIAN
(McColl 2, Browning 2)
Shaw, McNair, Dodds, Young,
Johnstone, McMaster, McAtee,
Gallacher, McColl, McMenemy,
Browning

1923
CELTIC 1-0 HIBERNIAN
(Cassidy)
Shaw, McNair, W. McStay, J McStay,
Cringan, McFarlane, McAtee,
Gallacher, Cassidy, McLean, Connolly

1925
CELTIC 2-1 DUNDEE
(Gallacher, McGrory)
Shevlin, W McStay, Hilley, Wilson,
J McStay, McFarlane, Connolly,
Gallacher, McGrory, A Thomson,
McLean

1927
CELTIC 3-1 EAST FIFE
(McLean, Connolly, Robertson og)
J Thomson, W McStay, Hilley,
Wilson, J McStay, McFarlane,
Connolly, A Thomson, McInally,
John McMenemy, McLean

1931
CELTIC 4-2 MOTHERWELL
(R Thomson 2, McGrory 2)
J Thomson, Cook, McGonagle,
Wilson, J McStay, Geatons,
R Thomson, A Thomson, McGrory,
Scarff, Napier

1933
CELTIC 1-0 MOTHERWELL
(McGrory)
Kennaway, Hogg, McGonagle,
Wilson, J McStay, Geatons,
R Thomson, A Thomson,
McGrory, Napier, H O'Donnell

1937
CELTIC 2-1 ABERDEEN
(Crum, Buchan)
Kennaway, Hogg, Morrison, Geatons,
Lyon, Paterson, Delaney, Buchan,
McGrory, Crum, Murphy

1951
CELTIC 1-0 MOTHERWELL
(J McPhail)
Hunter, Fallon, Rollo, Evans, Boden,
Baillie, Weir, Collins, J McPhail,
Peacock, Tully

1954
CELTIC 2-1 ABERDEEN
(Fallon, Young og)
Bonnar, Haughney, Meechan,
Evans, Stein, Peacock, Higgins,
Fernie, Fallon, Tully, Mochan

1965
CELTIC 3-2 DUNFERMLINE ATH
(Auld 2, McNeill)
Fallon, Young, Gemmell,
Murdoch, McNeill, Clark,
Chalmers, Gallagher, Hughes,
Lennox, Auld

1967
CELTIC 2-0 ABERDEEN
(Wallace 2)
Simpson, Craig, Gemmell,
Murdoch, McNeill, Clark,
Johnstone, Wallace, Chalmers,
Auld, Lennox

1969
CELTIC 4-0 RANGERS
(McNeill, Lennox, Connelly,
Chalmers)
Fallon, Craig, Gemmell, Murdoch,
McNeill, Brogan (Clark), Connelly,
Chalmers, Wallace, Lennox, Auld

1971
CELTIC 2-1 RANGERS
(Macari, Hood)
Williams, Craig, Brogan, Connelly,
McNeill, Hay, Johnstone, Macari,
Hood (Wallace), Callaghan, Lennox

1972
CELTIC 6-1 HIBERNIAN
(Deans 3, Macari 2, McNeill)
Williams, Craig, Brogan, Murdoch,
McNeill, Connelly, Johnstone,
Deans, Macari, Dalglish, Callaghan

1974
CELTIC 3-0 DUNDEE UNITED

(Murray, Hood, Deans)
Connaghan, McGrain (Callaghan),
Brogan, Murray, McNeill,
P McCluskey, Johnstone, Hood,
Deans, Hay, Dalglish

1975
CELTIC 3-1 AIRDRIE

(Wilson 2, P McCluskey)
Latchford, McGrain, Lynch, Murray,
McNeill, P McCluskey, Hood,
Glavin, Dalglish, Lennox, Wilson

1977
CELTIC 1-0 RANGERS

(Lynch)
Latchford, McGrain, Lynch,
Stanton, MacDonald, Aitken,
Dalglish, Edvaldsson, Craig,
Wilson, Conn

1980
CELTIC 1-0 RANGERS

(G McCluskey)
Latchford, Sneddon, McGrain, Aitken,
Conroy, MacLeod, Provan, Doyle
(Lennox), G McCluskey, Burns, McGarvey

1985
CELTIC 2-1 DUNDEE UNITED

(Provan, McGarvey)
Bonner, W McStay, McGrain, Aitken,
McAdam, MacLeod, Provan, P McStay
(O'Leary), Johnston, Burns (McClair),
McGarvey

1988
CELTIC 2-1 DUNDEE UNITED

(McAvennie 2)
McKnight, Morris, Rogan, Aitken,
McCarthy, Whyte (Stark), Miller,
P McStay, McAvennie, Walker (McGhee),
Burns

Celtic players celebrate winning the Scottish Cup in 1974

1989
CELTIC 1-0 RANGERS
(Miller)
Bonner, Morris, Rogan, Aitken, McCarthy, Whyte, Grant, P McStay, Miller, Burns, McGhee

1995
CELTIC 1-0 AIRDRIE
(van Hooijdonk)
Bonner, Boyd, McKinlay, Vata, McNally, Grant, McLaughlin, P McStay, van Hooijdonk (Falconer), Donnelly (O'Donnell), Collins

2001
CELTIC 3-0 HIBERNIAN
(McNamara, Larsson 2)
Douglas, Agathe, Mjallby, Vega, Valgaeren, Lambert (Boyd), Lennon, Moravcik (McNamara), Larsson, Sutton, Thompson (Johnson)

2004
CELTIC 3-1 DUNFERMLINE ATH
(Larsson 2, Petrov)
Marshall, Agathe, Varga, Balde, McNamara, Petrov, Lennon, Thompson, Pearson (Wallace), Larsson, Sutton

2005
CELTIC 1-0 DUNDEE UNITED
(Thompson)
Douglas, Agathe, Varga, Balde, McNamara, Petrov, Lennon, Thompson (McGeady), Bellamy, Hartson (Valgaeren), Sutton

2007
CELTIC 1-0 DUNFERMLINE ATH
(Perrier-Doumbe)

Boruc, Perrier-Doumbe, Pressley, McManus, Naylor, Nakamura, Lennon (Caldwell), Hartley, McGeady, Miller (Beattie), Vennegoor of Hesselink

2011
CELTIC 3-0 MOTHERWELL
(Ki Sung Yueng, Craigan og, Mulgrew)
Forster, Wilson, Loovens, Majstorovic, Izaguirre, Brown, Ki Sung Yueng, Mulgrew, Commons (Forrest), Samaras (Stokes), Hooper (McCourt)

Pierre van Hooijdonk was the match winner in 1995

SCOTTISH CUP RECORD v ALL OPPONENTS

Team	P	W	D	L	F	A	Team	P	W	D	L	F	A
5th KRV	1	1	0	0	7	0	Hibernian	22	13	7	2	41	11
6th GRV	1	1	0	0	8	1	Hurlford	2	2	0	0	10	0
Abercorn	0	0	0	0	0	0	Inverness Caledonian	1	1	0	0	6	0
Aberdeen	29	14	7	8	39	24	Inverness CT	5	3	0	2	7	6
Airdrieonians	14	11	3	0	39	14	Inverness Thistle	1	1	0	0	6	0
Albion Rovers	7	6	1	0	29	5	Keith	1	1	0	0	6	1
Alloa Athletic	4	4	0	0	13	0	Kilmarnock	19	11	3	5	41	16
Arbroath	5	5	0	0	20	3	Kilmarnock Athletic	1	1	0	0	3	0
Arthurlie	3	2	0	1	14	5	Leith Athletic	1	1	0	0	4	2
Ayr United	5	4	1	0	13	4	Linthouse	1	1	0	0	3	1
Bathgate	1	1	0	0	3	1	Livingston	2	2	0	0	7	2
Berwick Rangers	4	4	0	0	11	0	Lochgelly United	2	0	0	0	6	2
Bo'ness	3	3	0	0	15	3	Meadowbank Thistle	1	1	0	0	3	0
Brechin City	2	2	0	0	9	3	Montrose	7	7	0	0	35	4
Burntisland Shipyard	1	1	0	0	8	3	Morton	14	11	2	1	30	7
Carfin Shamrock	2	1	1	0	5	3	Motherwell	29	16	8	5	59	32
Clyde	24	13	7	4	41	17	Nithsdale Wanderers	1	1	0	0	5	0
Clydebank 1	0	0	0	0	0	0	Partick Thistle	9	7	2	0	27	7
Clydebank 2	6	6	0	0	24	3	Peebles Rovers	2	0	0	0	7	0
Cowdenbeath	2	2	0	0	8	1	Peterhead	1	1*	0	0	3	0
Cowlairs	2	2	0	0	12	1	Port Glasgow Ath	4	4	0	0	15	3
Dalbeattie Star	1	1	0	0	6	0	Queen of the South	5	4	1	0	18	3
Dumbarton	7	6	0	1	20	7	Queen's Park	12	9	0	3	31	20
Dumfries	1	1	0	0	2	1	Raith Rovers	8	8	0	0	27	7
Dundee	22	16	4	2	46	14	Rangers	48	23	9	16	73	61
Our Boys (Dundee)	1	1	0	0	3	1	Ross County	2	1	0	1	2	2
Dundee United	15	12	1	2	36	16	Royal Albert	1	1	0	0	3	0
Dunfermline Ath	21	15	4	2	46	16	St Bernard's	5	5	0	0	24	2
Duns	1	1	0	0	4	0	St Johnstone	6	5	0	1	15	7
East Fife	9	8	1	0	29	9	St Mirren	29	16	7	6	54	34
East Stirlingshire	4	4	0	0	10	1	Shettleston	1	1	0	0	5	1
Elgin City	2	0	0	0	9	1	Solway Star	1	1	0	0	2	0
Eyemouth United	2	0	0	0	7	0	Stenhousemuir	2	1	1	0	3	1
Falkirk	11	8	1	2	20	11	Stirling Albion	8	7	1	0	30	8
Forfar Athletic	3	3	0	0	9	1	Stranraer	3	3	0	0	9	1
Forres Mechanics	1	1	0	0	5	0	Third Lanark	16	10	3	3	42	21
Gala Fairydean	1	1	0	0	6	0	Thornliebank	1	1	0	0	3	0
Galston	1	1	0	0	1	0	Vale of Leven	1	1	0	0	3	0
Hamilton Academical	7	5	1	1	13	6	Wishaw Thistle	1	1	0	0	6	2
Hearts	29	17	5	7	57	35	Whitehill Welfare	1	1	0	0	3	0

FIRST AND LAST – SCOTTISH CUP

The first and last Scottish Cup games in the Hoops of four Celtic legends…

JIMMY QUINN

First

Celtic 1-0
St Mirren
23/03/1901

THE legendary Jimmy Quinn took his Scottish Cup bow at the semi-final stage when a 17,000 crowd at Celtic Park saw a Johnny Campbell goal give Celtic a 1-0 win. Quinn had only made his full debut just four days earlier against the same side and scored in a 4-3 league win at Paisley. Celtic were going for their third consecutive Scottish Cup triumph but, although Quinn scored in the final, they lost 4-3 to Hearts at Ibrox.

Last

Celtic 2-0 Clyde
10/02/14

JIMMY QUINN would go on to win five Scottish Cup winner's medals and would play in another three finals – one of those being the 1909 final when the trophy was withheld. His final Scottish Cup game came in a first-round replay against Clyde when Patsy Gallacher scored twice and the Hoops went on to win the trophy with a 4-1 win over Hibernian. Quinn also only played one league game that season and played a handful the following term but, by then, the Scottish Cup was suspended for the First Word War.

PATSY GALLACHER

First

Hearts 0-3 Celtic
30/03/12

THE Irishman's first Scottish Cup game was at the semi-final stage when the Celts took to the field against Hearts at Ibrox in front of a 43,000 crowd. Jimmy McMenemy struck twice and John Brown hit another to take Celtic back to the same venue a few weeks later in the final. This time Celtic were up against Clyde and the 46,000 crowd saw Gallacher score in Celtic's 2-0 win.

Last

Dundee 1-2 Celtic
11/04/25

WHAT better way to finish your Scottish Cup career than by having the last game named after you? The 1925 showdown will forever be known as The Patsy Gallacher Final after his wonder-goal prompted a dramatic comeback win. Dundee scored first and young Jimmy McGrory, who had scored in every round so far, scored the winner with five minutes to go. It was

Gallacher's equaliser, though, a solo goal where he beat player after player before somersaulting into the net with the ball between his feet, that has been carved into the Celtic psyche.

BILLY McNEILL

First
St Mirren 1-1 Celtic
13/02/60

THE young Billy McNeill was still 19-years-old when he took his Scottish Cup bow in what turned out to be a marathon three-game epic – the final 90 minutes of which turned out to be Fergus McCann's favourite Celtic game. Love Street thronged with 36,220 people for this 1-1 draw and 11 days later, 38,000 turned up for a thrilling 4-4 draw at Celtic Park. Just five days later, another 51,000 returned to the same venue and witnessed Neilly Mochan score five times in a 5-2 win.

Last
Airdrie 1-3 Celtic
03/05/75

WHEN Celtic went out at the semi-final stage in Billy McNeill's first Scottish Cup, little did he know that he would play in 11 of the next 15 finals, score in three of them and pick up SEVEN winner's medals. And his final Celtic game was the Scottish Cup final of 1975 when, after defeating Airdrie 3-1, he raised the trophy for the last time and then announced his retirement from the playing side of the game.

PAUL McSTAY

First
Celtic 4-0 Queen of the South
23/01/82

THIS was also Paul McStay's full Celtic bow and although fellow debutant, John Halpin, grabbed some of the limelight by scoring in the 4-0 win, it was the stylish play of the young midfielder that caught the eye. A week later he marked his league debut by scoring against Aberdeen in a 3-1 win at Pittodrie and another McStay legend was in the making at Celtic Park.

Last
Celtic 2-0 Rangers
03/03/97

IN a season hampered by injury, Paul McStay went out on a high as far as the Scottish Cup was concerned as the visitors for the quarter-final tie were Rangers. Malky Mackay and Paolo Di Canio were the Celts who got the goals in a 2-0 win to knock the Ibrox side out. McStay bowed out of the competition with four winner's medals, the last of those coming when he captained the side to victory in 1995.

SCOTTISH CUP WINNERS

1873/74
Queen's Park 2-0 Clydesdale
1874/75
Queen's Park 3-0 Renton
1875/76
Queen's Park 1-1 3rd Lanark RV
(R) Queen's Park 2-0 3rd Lanark RV
1876/77
Vale of Leven 1-1 Rangers
(R) Vale of Leven 1-1 Rangers
(SR) Vale of Leven 3-2 Rangers
1877/78
Vale of Leven 1-0 3rd Lanark RV
1878/79
Vale of Leven 1-1 Rangers
(R) Vale of Leven (walkover)
1879/80
Queen's Park 3-0 Thornliebank
1880/81
Queen's Park 2-1 Dumbarton
 (R) Queen's Park 3-1 Dumbarton
1881/82
Queen's Park 2-2 Dumbarton
(R) Queen's Park 4-1 Dumbarton
1882/83
Dumbarton 2-2 Vale of Leven
(R) Dumbarton 2-1 Vale of Leven
1883/84
Queen's Park (won) v Vale of Leven
1884/85
Renton 0-0 Vale of Leven
(R) Renton 3-1 Vale of Leven
1885/86
Queen's Park 3-1 Renton
1886/87
Hibernian 2-1 Dumbarton
1887/88
Renton 6-1 Cambuslang

1888/89
3rd Lanark RV 3-0 Celtic
(R) 3rd Lanark RV 2-1 Celtic
1889/90
Queen's Park 1-1 Vale of Leven
(R) Queen's Park 2-1 Vale of Leven
1890/91
Hearts 1-0 Dumbarton
1891/92
Celtic 1-0 Queen's Park
(R) Celtic 5-1 Queen's Park
1892/93
Queen's Park 0-1 Celtic
(R) Queen's Park 2-1 Celtic
1893/94
Rangers 3-1 Celtic
1894/95
St Bernard's 2-1 Renton
1895/96
Hearts 3-1 Hibernian
1896/97
Rangers 5-1 Dumbarton
1897/98
Rangers 2-0 Kilmarnock
1898/99
Celtic 2-0 Rangers
1899/1900
Celtic 4-3 Queen's Park
1900/01
Hearts 4-3 Celtic
1901/02
Hibernian 1-0 Celtic
1902/03
Rangers 1-1 Hearts
(R) Rangers 0-0 Hearts
(SR) Rangers 2-0 Hearts
1903/04
Celtic 3-2 Rangers

1904/05
Third Lanark 0-0 Rangers
(R) Third Lanark 3-1 Rangers
1905/06
Hearts 1-0 Third Lanark
1906/07
Celtic 3-0 Hearts
1907/08
Celtic 5-1 St Mirren
1909/10
Dundee 2-2 Clyde
(R) Dundee 0-0 Clyde
(SR) Dundee 2-1 Clyde
1910/11
Celtic 0-0 Hamilton
(R) Celtic 2-0 Hamilton
1911/12
Celtic 2-0 Clyde
1912/13
Falkirk 2-0 Raith Rovers
1913/14
Celtic 0-0 Hibernian
(R) Celtic 4-1 Hibernian
1919/20
Kilmarnock 3-2 Albion Rovers
1920/21
Partick Thistle 1-0 Rangers
1921/22
Morton 1-0 Rangers
1922/23
Celtic 1-0 Hibernian
1923/24
Airdrie 2-0 Hibernian
1924/25
Celtic 2-1 Dundee
1925/26
St Mirren 2-0 Celtic
1926/27
Celtic 3-1 East Fife

1927/28
Rangers 4-0 Celtic
1928/29
Kilmarnock 1-0 Rangers
1929/30
Rangers 0-0 Partick Thistle
(R) Rangers 2-1 Partick Thistle
1930/31
Celtic 2-2 Motherwell
(R) Celtic 4-2 Motherwell
1931/32
Rangers 1-1 Kilmarnock
(R) Rangers 3-0 Kilmarnock
1932/33
Celtic 1-0 Motherwell
1933/34
Rangers 5-0 St Mirren
1934/35
Rangers 2-1 Hamilton
1935/36
Rangers 1-0 Third Lanark
1936/37
Celtic 2-1 Aberdeen
1937/38
East Fife 1-1 Kilmarnock
(R) East Fife 4-2 Kilmarnock
1938/39
Clyde 4-0 Motherwell
1946/47
Aberdeen 2-1 Hibernian
1947/48
Rangers 1-1 Morton
(R) Rangers 1-0 Morton
1948/49
Rangers 4-1 Clyde
1949/50
Rangers 3-0 East Fife
1950/51
Celtic 1-0 Motherwell

SCOTTISH CUP WINNERS continued...

1951/52
Motherwell 4-0 Dundee
1952/53
Rangers 1-1 Aberdeen
(R) Rangers 1-0 Aberdeen
1953/54
Celtic 2-1 Aberdeen
1954/55
Clyde 1-1 Celtic
(R) Clyde 1-0 Celtic
1955/56
Hearts 3-1 Celtic
1956/57
Falkirk 1-1 Kilmarnock
(R)Falkirk 2-1 Kilmarnock
1957/58
Clyde 1-0 Hibernian
1958/59
St Mirren 3-1 Aberdeen
1959/60
Rangers 2-0 Kilmarnock
1960/61
Dunfermline 0-0 Celtic
(R) Dunfermline 2-0 Celtic
1961/62
Rangers 2-0 St Mirren
1962/63
Rangers 1-1 Celtic
(R) Rangers 3-0 Celtic
1963/64
Rangers 3-1 Dundee
1964/65
Celtic 3-2 Dunfermline
1965/66
Rangers 0-0 Celtic
(R) Rangers 1-0 Celtic
1966/67
Celtic 2-0 Aberdeen

1967/68
Dunfermline 3-1 Hearts
1968/69
Celtic 4-0 Rangers
1969/70
Aberdeen 3-1 Celtic
1970/71
Celtic 1-1 Rangers
(R) Celtic 2-1 Rangers
1971/72
Celtic 6-1 Hibernian
1972/73
Rangers 3-2 Celtic
1973/74
Celtic 3-0 Dundee United
1974/75
Celtic 3-1 Airdrie
1975/76
Rangers 3-1 Hearts
1976/77
Celtic 1-0 Rangers
1977/78
Rangers 2-1 Aberdeen
1978/79
Rangers 0-0 Hibernian
(R) Rangers 0-0 Hibernian
(SR) Rangers 3-2 Hibernian
1979/80
Celtic 1-0 Rangers

Billy McNeill wins possession in the 1972 final

1980/81
Rangers 0-0 Dundee United
(R) Rangers 4-1 Dundee United
1981/82
Aberdeen 4-1 Rangers
1982/83
Aberdeen 1-0 Rangers
1983/84
Aberdeen 2-1 Celtic
1984/85
Celtic 2-1 Dundee United
1985/86
Aberdeen 3-0 Hearts
1986/87
St Mirren 1-0 Dundee United
1987/88
Celtic 2-1 Dundee United
1988/89
Celtic 1-0 Rangers
1989/90
Aberdeen 0-0 Celtic
(Aberdeen win on penalties)
1990/91
Motherwell 4-3 Dundee United
1991/92
Rangers 2-1 Airdrie
1992/93
Rangers 2-1 Aberdeen
1993/94
Dundee United 1-0 Rangers
1994/95
Celtic 1-0 Airdrie
1995/96
Rangers 5-1 Hearts
1996/97
Kilmarnock 1-0 Falkirk
1997/98
Hearts 2-1 Rangers

1998/99
Rangers 1-0 Celtic
1999/2000
Rangers 4-0 Aberdeen
2000/01
Celtic 3-0 Hibernian
2001/02
Rangers 3-2 Celtic
2002/03
Rangers 1-0 Dundee
2003/04
Celtic 3-1 Dunfermline
2004/05
Celtic 1-0 Dundee United
2005/06
Hearts 1-1 Gretna
(Hearts win on penalties)
2006/07
Celtic 1-0 Dunfermline
2007/08
Rangers 3-2 Queen of the South
2008/09
Rangers 1-0 Falkirk
2009/10
Dundee United 3-0 Ross County
2010/11
Celtic 3-0 Motherwell
2011/12
Hearts 5-1 Hibernian

Paul Lambert and Tom Boyd lift the trophy in 2001

LEAGUE CUP FINAL WINNING TEAMS

1956/57
CELTIC 3-0 PARTICK THISTLE
(B McPhail 2, Collins)
Beattie, Haughney, Fallon, Evans,
Jack, Peacock, Tully, Collins,
B McPhail, Fernie, Mochan

1957/58
CELTIC 7-1 RANGERS
(B McPhail 3, Mochan 2, Wilson,
Fernie)
Beattie, Donnelly, Fallon, Fernie,
Evans, Peacock, Tully, Collins,
B McPhail, Wilson, Mochan

1965/66
CELTIC 2-1 RANGERS
(Hughes 2)
Simpson, Young, Gemmell, Murdoch,
McNeill, Clark, Johnstone, Gallagher,
McBride, Lennox, Hughes

1966/67
CELTIC 1-0 RANGERS
(Lennox)
Simpson, Gemmell, O'Neill,
Murdoch, McNeill, Clark,
Johnstone, Lennox, McBride,
Auld, Hughes (Chalmers)

The 1957/58 League Cup-winning team

1967/68
CELTIC 5-3 DUNDEE
(Chalmers 2, Hughes, Lennox,
Wallace)
Simpson, Craig, Gemmell, Murdoch,
McNeill, Clark, Chalmers, Lennox,
Wallace, Auld (O'Neill), Hughes

1968/69
CELTIC 6-2 HIBERNIAN
(Lennox 3, Wallace, Auld, Craig)
Fallon, Craig, Gemmell (Clark),
Murdoch, McNeill, Brogan,
Johnstone, Wallace, Chalmers, Auld,
Lennox

1969/70
CELTIC 1-0 ST JOHNSTONE
(Auld)
Fallon, Craig, Hay, Murdoch, McNeill,
Brogan, Callaghan, Hood, Hughes,
Chalmers (Johnstone), Auld

1974/75
CELTIC 6-3 HIBERNIAN
(Deans 3, Wilson, Murray, Johnstone)
Hunter, McGrain, Brogan, Murray,
McNeill, P. McCluskey, Johnstone,
Dalglish, Deans, Hood, Wilson

1982/83
CELTIC 2-1 RANGERS
Nicholas, MacLeod)
Bonner, McGrain, Sinclair, Aitken,
McAdam, MacLeod, Provan,
P McStay (Reid), McGarvey, Burns,
Nicholas

1997/98
CELTIC 3-0 DUNDEE UNITED
(Rieper, Larsson, Burley)
Gould, Boyd, Mahe, McNamara
(Annoni), Rieper, Stubbs, Larsson,
Burley, Thom (Donnelly), Wieghorst,
Blinker (Lambert)

Charlie Nicholas wheels away after netting in the 1982/83 derby final

1999/2000
CELTIC 2-0 ABERDEEN
(Riseth, Johnson)
Gould, Boyd, Riseth, Mjallby, Mahe, McNamara, Wieghorst, Petrov, Moravcik (Stubbs), Johnson (Berkovic), Viduka

2000/01
CELTIC 3-0 KILMARNOCK
(Larsson 3)
Gould, Healy, Mjallby, Vega, Valgaeren, Lambert, Lennon, Moravcik (Smith), Larsson, Sutton, Petta (Crainey) (Boyd)

2005/06
CELTIC 3-0 DUNFERMLINE ATH
(Zurawski, Maloney, Dublin)
Boruc, Telfer, Balde, McManus, Wallace, Nakamura, Keane (Dublin), Lennon, Petrov, Maloney, Zurawski

2008/09
CELTIC 2-0 RANGERS
(O'Dea, McGeady)
Boruc, Hinkel, Loovens, McManus, O'Dea (Wilson), Brown, Hartley (Samaras) (Vennegoor of Hesselink), Nakamura, Caldwell, McDonald, McGeady

Henrik Larsson hit a treble in the 2001 final

LEAGUE CUP RECORD v ALL OPPONENTS

Team	P	W	D	L	F	A	Team	P	W	D	L	F	A
Aberdeen	27	14	4	9	44	34	Heart of Midlothian	20	12	1	7	44	26
Airdrieonians	21	13	5	3	45	19	Hibernian	22	11	5	6	55	37
Albion Rovers	2	2	0	0	6	0	Inverness CT	2	2	0	0	10	2
Alloa Athletic	3	3	0	0	14	2	Kilmarnock	10	6	2	2	15	6
Arbroath	9	8	1	0	36	8	Livingston	2	2	0	0	6	0
Ayr United	13	11	1	1	43	13	Montrose	2	1	1	0	4	2
Berwick Rangers	1	1	0	0	7	0	Morton	9	7	0	2	23	7
Brechin City	3	2	1	0	8	0	Motherwell	16	10	3	3	28	20
Clyde	12	11	0	1	37	14	Partick Thistle	23	14	4	5	48	24
Clydebank 2	2	2	0	0	11	2	Queen of the South	7	6	1	0	18	7
Cowdenbeath	2	2	0	0	10	1	Raith Rovers	12	9	2	1	39	12
Dumbarton	9	7	2	0	32	8	Rangers	47	21	2	24	70	67
Dundee	21	12	2	7	40	27	Ross County	1	1	0	0	2	0
Dundee United	25	14	6	5	36	19	St Johnstone	7	4	0	3	9	8
Dunfermline Ath	9	8	0	1	35	10	St Mirren	14	11	0	3	39	16
East Fife	12	7	3	2	27	11	Stenhousemuir	2	2	0	0	3	0
Falkirk	13	10	3	0	39	11	Stirling Albion	11	9	1	1	32	5
Forfar Athletic	3	2	1	0	8	3	Stranraer	2	2	0	0	7	3
Hamilton Academical	10	9	1	0	40	11	Third Lanark	12	9	2	1	29	11

Celtic dedicate the 2006 League Cup win to
Jimmy Johnstone, who had recently passed away

FIRST AND LAST - LEAGUE CUP

The first and last League Cup games in the Hoops of four Celtic legends…

BILLY McPHAIL

First
Aberdeen 1-2 Celtic
11/08/56

CLOSE-SEASON signing, Billy McPhail, who joined the club on the same day big brother John left, took his Celtic bow in this League Cup sectional game at Pittodrie where goals from Willie Fernie and John Higgins helped the Hoops to a 2-1 win. The Celts would go on to reach the final for the first time and McPhail scored twice in the 3-0 replay win over Partick Thistle.

Last
Celtic 7-1 Rangers
19/10/57

WHERE do we start? Celtic beat their greatest rivals 7-1 in the League Cup final and Billy McPhail netted a hat-trick. In the close season trial game of 1958, McPhail's knee gave in and he had to retire from the game. However, in those two short seasons with Celtic he had played in two winning League Cup finals and scored five goals in those games. In all, he scored 22 goals in only 20 League Cup games – not a bad return.

BERTIE AULD

First
Airdrie 1-2 Celtic
24/08/57

THE inimitable Bertie Auld's first League Cup game was his Celtic bow proper following a Charity Cup game at the end of the previous season. Eric Smith and Willie Fernie got the goals in a 2-1 win but, although Bertie would play in six successive League Cup games up until the semi-final, he missed out on the 7-1 final win over Rangers.

Last
25/10/70
Celtic 1-0 St Johnstone

THE man with a wit as cutting as any of his passes won four League Cup winner's medals, all in a row, and the last of those came in his final game in the competition. He had scored in the previous final, the 6-2 win over Hibernian, but the 1970 final win in front of 73,067 was all down to him as it was Bertie's solitary goal after only two minutes that was the difference between the Hoops and St Johnstone on the day.

JIMMY JOHNSTONE

First
10/08/63
Celtic 0-3 Rangers

OKAY, this wasn't the best of starts for Jimmy Johnstone's League Cup story but this was a young side on a learning curve and Jinky, along with his fellow Celtic team-mates, was to have the upper hand over Rangers in the League Cup, and just about any other competition you care to mention, well into the following decade. Jinky himself would win five League Cup winner's medals over the forthcoming years.

Last
26/10/74
Celtic 6-3 Hibernian

JINKY had played in the 1968/69 final when Celtic beat Hibernian 6-2 and his final game featured the same opposition in 1974 when Hibs pushed the boat out a bit and tightened the scoreline to 6-3 this time. And it was Jinky who set the ball rolling with the opener in the sixth minute and much of Celtic's superiority that afternoon was down to his foraging runs – even Dixie Deans who scored a hat-trick (along with Hibs' Joe Harper) couldn't hog all the limelight that afternoon.

SHUNSUKE NAKAMURA

First
Celtic 2-1 Falkirk
21/09/06

THE Japanese midfielder's first League Cup tie saw Falkirk visit Celtic Park and it was the visitors who took the lead but goals from Maciej Zurawski and John Hartson pulled the tie in Celtic's favour. Nakamura won his first medal with Celtic later that season as he played in the side that beat Dunfermline 3-0 in the League Cup final which followed earlier wins over Rangers and Motherwell in the competition. The win was dedicated to Jimmy Johnstone who had passed away earlier that week.

Last
Celtic 2-0 Rangers
15/03/09

IN his final League Cup game for the Hoops, Nakamura walked away with another winner's medal, the sixth from all competitions in his four-season stay with Celtic. Rangers provided the opposition and the 90 minutes finished 0-0 to take the game into extra-time. It was a Nakamura free-kick that teed up Darren O'Dea to score the opener just two minutes into the extra period and the scorer's Republic of Ireland team-mate, Aiden McGeady tied things up at the end with a penalty after he had been brought down.

LEAGUE CUP WINNERS

1946/47
Rangers 4-0 Aberdeen
1947/48
East Fife 0-0 Falkirk
(R) East Fife 4-1 Falkirk
1948/49
Rangers 2-0 Raith Rovers
1949/50
East Fife 3-0 Dunfermline
1950/51
Motherwell 3-0 Hibernian
1951/52
Dundee 3-2 Rangers
1952/53
Dundee 2-0 Kilmarnock
1953/54
East Fife 3-2 Partick Thistle

1954/55
Hearts 4-2 Motherwell
1955/56
Aberdeen 2-1 St Mirren
1956/57
Celtic 0-0 Partick Thistle
(R) Celtic 3-0 Partick Thistle
1957/58
Celtic 7-1 Rangers
1958/59
Hearts 5-1 Partick Thistle
1959/60
Hearts 2-1 Third Lanark
1960/61
Rangers 2-0 Kilmarnock

Celtic retained the League Cup in season 1957/58... and how

1961/62
Rangers 1-1 Hearts
(R) Rangers 3-1 Hearts
1962/63
Hearts 1-0 Kilmarnock
1963/64
Rangers 5-0 Morton
1964/65
Rangers 2-1 Celtic
1965/66
Celtic 2-1 Rangers
1966/67
Celtic 1-0 Rangers
1967/68
Celtic 5-3 Dundee
1968/69
Celtic 6-2 Hibernian
1969/70
Celtic 1-0 St Johnstone
1970/71
Rangers 1-0 Celtic
1971/72
Partick Thistle 4-1 Celtic
1972/73
Hibernian 2-1 Celtic
1973/74
Dundee 1-0 Celtic
1974/75
Celtic 6-3 Hibernian
1975/76
Rangers 1-0 Celtic

1976/77
Aberdeen 2-1 Celtic
1977/78
Rangers 2-1 Celtic
1978/79
Rangers 2-1 Aberdeen
1979/80
Dundee United 0-0 Aberdeen
(R) Dundee United 3-0 Aberdeen
1980/81
Dundee United 3-0 Dundee
1981/82
Rangers 2-1 Dundee United
1982/83
Celtic 2-1 Rangers
1983/84
Rangers 3-2 Celtic
1984/85
Rangers 1-0 Dundee United
1985/86
Aberdeen 3-0 Hibernian
1986/87
Rangers 2-1 Celtic

Jimmy Johnstone is mobbed after scoring in the 1974/75 final

LEAGUE CUP WINNERS continued...

1987/88
Rangers 3-3 Aberdeen
(Rangers win on penalties)
1988/89
Rangers 3-2 Aberdeen
1989/90
Aberdeen 2-1 Rangers
1990/91
Rangers 2-1 Celtic
1991/92
Hibernian 2-0 Dunfermline
1992/93
Rangers 2-1 Aberdeen
1993/94
Rangers 2-1 Hibernian
1994/95
Raith Rovers 2-2 Celtic
(Raith Rovers win on penalties)
1995/96
Aberdeen 2-0 Dundee
1996/97
Rangers 4-3 Hearts
1997/98
Celtic 3-0 Dundee United
1998/99
Rangers 2-1 St Johnstone
1999/2000
Celtic 2-0 Aberdeen
2000/01
Celtic 3-0 Kilmarnock
2001/02
Rangers 4-0 Ayr United

2002/03
Rangers 2-1 Celtic
2003/04
Livingston 2-0 Hibernian
2004/05
Rangers 5-1 Motherwell
2005/06
Celtic 3-0 Dunfermline
2006/07
Hibernian 5-1 Kilmarnock
2007/08
Rangers 2-2 Dundee United
(Rangers win on penalties)
2008/09
Celtic 2-0 Rangers
2009/10
Rangers 1-0 St Mirren
2010/11
Rangers 2-1 Celtic
2011/12
Kilmarnock 1-0 Celtic

Stephen McManus after beating Rangers 2-0 in 2009

CELTIC
IN EUROPE

CELTIC'S EUROPEAN RESULTS COUNTRY BY COUNTRY

(Celtic score first, * Denotes first tie played, Nationality based on current borders)

ALBANIA

Season	Comp	Stage	Opposition	H	A	Agg	Notes
1979/80	EC	R1	Partizan Tirana	4-1	0-1*	4-2	
TOTAL				*4-1*	*0-1*	*4-2*	

AUSTRIA

Season	Comp	Stage	Opposition	H	A	Agg	Notes
2009/10	Europa	GS	Rapid Vienna	1-1*	3-3	4-4	
1997/98	UEFA	Q2	Tirol Innsbruck	6-3	1-2*	7-5	
1984/85	CWC	R2	Rapid Vienna	0-1	1-3*	1-4	

Home game played at Old Trafford following 3-0 'win' for Celtic in Glasgow being struck from records

1977/78	EC	R2	Tirol Innsbruck	2-1*	0-3	2-4	
TOTAL				*9-6*	*5-11*	*14-17*	

BELGIUM

Season	Comp	Stage	Opposition	H	A	Agg	Notes
2003/04	EC	GS	Anderlecht	3-1	0-1*	3-2	
1991/92	UEFA	R1	Germinal Ekeren	2-0*	1-1	3-1	
1984/85	CWC	R1	KAA Gent	3-0	0-1*	3-1	
TOTAL				*8-0*	*1-3*	*9-4*	

CROATIA

Season	Comp	Stage	Opposition	H	A	Agg	Notes
1998/99	UEFA	Q2	Croatia Zagreb	1-0*	0-3	1-3	
1963/64	CWC	R2	Croatia Zagreb	3-0*	1-2	4-2	
TOTAL				*4-0*	*1-5*	*5-5*	

CZECH REPUBLIC

Season	Comp	Stage	Opposition	H	A	Agg	Notes
2003/04	UEFA	R3	FK Teplice	3-0*	0-1	3-1	Following EC elimination
1966/67	EC	SF	Dukla Prague	3-1*	0-0	3-1	
TOTAL				*6-1*	*0-1*	*6-2*	

DENMARK

Season	Comp	Stage	Opposition	H	A	Agg	Notes
2008/09	EC	GS	Aalborg	0-0*	1-2	1-2	
2006/07	EC	GS	FC Copenhagen	1-0*	1-3	2-3	
1983/84	UEFA	R1	AGF Aarhus	1-0*	4-1	5-1	
1973/74	EC	R2	Vejle BK	0-0*	1-0	1-0	
1971/72	EC	R1	BK1903 Copenhagen	3-0	1-2*	4-2	
1965/66	CWC	R2	AGF Aarhus	2-0	1-0*	3-0	
TOTAL				*7-0*	*9-8*	*16-8*	

ENGLAND

Season	Comp	Stage	Opposition	H	A	Agg	Notes
2009/10	EC	PO	Arsenal	0-2*	1-3	1-5	
2008/09	EC	GS	Manchester United	1-1	0-3*	1-4	
2006/07	EC	GS	Manchester United	1-0	2-3*	3-3	
2002/03	UEFA	QF	Liverpool	1-1*	2-0	3-1	*Following EC elimination*
2002/03	UEFA	R2	Blackburn Rovers	1-0*	2-0	3-0	
1997/98	UEFA	R1	Liverpool	2-2*	0-0	2-2	*Lost on away goals*
1983/84	EC	R3	Nottingham Forest	1-2	0-0*	1-2	
1969/70	EC	SF	Leeds United	2-1	1-0*	3-1	
1965/66	CWC	SF	Liverpool	1-0*	0-2	1-2	
TOTAL				**10-9**	**8-11**	**18-20**	

FINLAND

Season	Comp	Stage	Opposition	H	A	Agg	Notes
2000/01	UEFA	R1	HJK Helsinki	2-0*	1-2	3-2	
1973/74	EC	R1	Turku	3-0	6-1*	9-1	
1970/71	EC	R1	Kokkola	9-0*	5-0	14-0	
TOTAL				**14-0**	**12-3**	**26-3**	

FRANCE

Season	Comp	Stage	Opposition	H	A	Agg	Notes
2011/12	Europa	GS	Rennes	3-1	1-1*	4-2	
2003/04	EC	GS	Olympique Lyon	2-0*	2-3	4-3	
2000/01	UEFA	R2	Bordeaux	1-2	1-1*	2-3	
1999/00	UEFA	R2	Olympique Lyon	0-1	0-1*	0-2	
1995/96	CWC	R2	Paris Saint-Germain	0-3	0-1*	0-4	
1968/69	EC	R1	St Etienne	4-0	0-2*	4-2	
1966/67	EC	R2	Nantes	3-1	3-1*	6-2	
TOTAL				**13-8**	**7-10**	**20-18**	

GEORGIA

Season	Comp	Stage	Opposition	H	A	Agg	Notes
1995/96	CWC	R1	Dinamo Batumi	4-0	3-2*	7-2	
TOTAL				**4-0**	**3-2**	**7-2**	

GERMANY

Season	Comp	Stage	Opposition	H	A	Agg	Notes
2009/10	Europa	GS	SV Hamburg	0-1*	0-0	0-1	
2003/04	EC	GS	Bayern Munich	0-0	1-2*	1-2	
2002/03	UEFA	R4	VfB Stuttgart	3-1*	2-3	5-4	
1996/97	UEFA	R1	SV Hamburg	0-2*	0-2	0-4	
1992/93	UEFA	R2	Borussia Dortmund	1-2	0-1*	1-3	
1992/93	UEFA	R1	FC Cologne	3-0	0-2*	3-2	
1988/89	EC	R2	Werder Bremen	0-1*	0-0	0-1	
1987/88	UEFA	R1	Borussia Dortmund	2-1*	0-2	2-3	
1975/76	CWC	QF	FSV Zwickau	1-1*	0-1	1-2	
TOTAL				**10-9**	**3-13**	**13-22**	

GREECE

Season	Comp	Stage	Opposition	H	A	Agg	Notes
1974/75	EC	R1	Olympiakos Piraeus	1-1*	0-2	1-3	
TOTAL				*1-1*	*0-2*	*1-3*	

HOLLAND

Season	Comp	Stage	Opposition	H	A	Agg	Notes
2010/11	EL	Q3	FC Utrecht	2-0*	0-4	2-4	
2001/02	EC	Q3	Ajax	0-1	3-1*	3-2	
1982/83	EC	R1	Ajax	2-2*	2-1	4-3	
1970/71	EC	QF	Ajax	1-0	0-3*	1-3	
1969/70	EC	F	Feyenoord	Neutral		1-2(AET)	*1-1 90mins*
1965/66	CWC	R1	Go Ahead Deventer	1-0	6-0*	7-0	
TOTAL				*6-3*	*11-9*	*18-14*	

HUNGARY

Season	Comp	Stage	Opposition	H	A	Agg	Notes
2003/04	EC	Q2	MTK Hungaria	1-0	4-0*	5-0	
1988/89	EC	R1	Honved	4-0	0-1*	4-1	
1980/81	CWC	Q1	Diosgyor Miskolc	6-0*	1-2	7-2	
1972/73	EC	R2	Ujpest Dosza	2-1*	0-3	2-4	
1971/72	EC	QF	Ujpest Dosza	1-1	2-1*	3-2	
1963/64	CWC	SF	MTK Budapest	3-0*	0-4	3-4	
TOTAL				*17-2*	*7-11*	*24-13*	

ICELAND

Season	Comp	Stage	Opposition	H	A	Agg	Notes
1975/76	CWC	R1	Valur Reykjavik	7-0	2-0*	9-0	
TOTAL				*7-0*	*2-0*	*9-0*	

ISRAEL

Season	Comp	Stage	Opposition	H	A	Agg	Notes
2009/10	Europa	GS	Hapoel Tel Aviv	2-0	1-2*	3-2	
1999/00	UEFA	R1	Hapoel Tel-Aviv	2-0*	1-0	3-0	
TOTAL				*4-0*	*2-2*	*6-2*	

ITALY

Season	Comp	Stage	Opposition	H	A	Agg	Notes
2011/12	Europa	GS	Udinese	1-1*	1-1	2-2	
2007/08	EC	GS	AC Milan	2-1	0-1	2-2	
2006/07	EC	L16	AC Milan	0-0*	0-1	0-1(AET)	
2004/05	EC	R1	AC Milan	0-0	1-3*	1-3	
2001/02	EC	R1	Juventus	4-3	2-3*	6-6	
1981/82	EC	R1	Juventus	1-0*	0-2	1-2	
1971/72	EC	SF	Inter Milan	0-0	0-0*	0-0	*Lost 4-5 on penalties*
1969/70	EC	QF	Fiorentina	3-0*	0-1	3-1	
1968/69	EC	QF	AC Milan	0-1	0-0*	0-1	

ITALY cont...

Season	Comp	Stage	Opposition			Agg	Notes
1966/67	EC	F	Inter Milan	Neutral		2-1	
TOTAL				*11-6*	*4-12*	*17-19*	

LITHUANIA

Season	Comp	Stage	Opposition	H	A	Agg	Notes
2003/04	EC	Q2	FBK Kaunas	1-0	4-0*	5-0	*Following EC elimination*
2002/03	UEFA	R1	FK Suduva	8-1*	2-0	10-1	
TOTAL				*9-1*	*6-0*	*15-1*	

LUXEMBOURG

Season	Comp	Stage	Opposition	H	A	Agg	Notes
2000/01	UEFA	Q1	Jeunesse d'Esch	7-0	4-0*	11-0	
1977/78	EC	R1	Jeunesse d'Esch	5-0*	6-1	11-1	
TOTAL				*12-0*	*10-1*	*22-1*	

MALTA

Season	Comp	Stage	Opposition	H	A	Agg	Notes
1971/72	EC	R2	Sliema Wanderers	5-0*	2-1	7-1	
TOTAL				*5-0*	*2-1*	*7-1*	

NORWAY

Season	Comp	Stage	Opposition	H	A	Agg	Notes
2001/02	EC	R1	Rosenborg	1-0*	0-2	1-2	
1972/73	EC	R1	Rosenborg	2-1*	3-1	5-2	
TOTAL				*3-1*	*3-3*	*6-4*	

POLAND

Season	Comp	Stage	Opposition	H	A	Agg	Notes
1976/77	UEFA	R1	Wisla Krakow	2-2*	0-2	2-4	
TOTAL				*2-2*	*0-2*	*2-4*	

PORTUGAL

Season	Comp	Stage	Opposition	H	A	Agg	Notes
2010/11	EC	Q3	SC Braga	2-1	0-3*	2-4	
2007/08	EC	GS	Benfica	1-0	0-1*	1-1	
2006/07	EC	GS	Benfica	3-0*	0-3	3-3	
2002/03	UEFA	F	Porto	Neutral		2-3 (AET)	
2002/03	UEFA	SF	Boavista	1-1*	1-0	2-1	
2001/02	EC	R1	Porto	1-0*	0-3	1-3	
1998/99	UEFA	R1	Vitoria Guimaraes	2-1	2-1*	4-2	*Following EC elimination*
1993/94	UEFA	R2	Sporting Lisbon	1-0*	0-2	1-2	
1983/84	UEFA	R2	Sporting Lisbon	5-0	0-2*	5-2	
1975/76	CWC	R2	Boavista	3-1	0-0*	3-1	
1969/70	EC	R2	Benfica	3-0*	0-3	3-3	*Won on toss of coin*
1964/65	UEFA	R1	Leixoes	3-0	1-1*	4-1	
TOTAL				*25-4*	*4-19*	*31-26*	

REPUBLIC OF IRELAND

Season	Comp	Stage	Opposition	H	A	Agg	Notes
1998/99	EC	Q1	St Patrick's Athletic	0-0*	2-0	2-0	
1986/87	EC	R1	Shamrock Rovers	2-0	1-0*	3-0	
1979/80	EC	R2	Dundalk	3-2*	0-0	3-2	
1970/71	EC	R2	Waterford United	3-2	7-0*	10-2	
TOTAL				*8-4*	*10-0*	*18-4*	

ROMANIA

Season	Comp	Stage	Opposition	H	A	Agg	Notes
1980/81	CWC	R1	Politechnica Timisoara	2-1*	0-1	2-2	*Lost on away goals*
TOTAL				*2-1*	*0-1*	*2-2*	

RUSSIA

Season	Comp	Stage	Opposition	H	A	Agg	Notes
2009/10	EC	Q3	Dinamo Moscow	0-1*	2-0	2-1	
200708	EC	Q3	Spartak Moscow	1-1	1-1*	2-2	*Won on penalties*
TOTAL				*1-2*	*3-1*	*4-3*	

SLOVAKIA

Season	Comp	Stage	Opposition	H	A	Agg	Notes
2005/06	EC	Q2	Artmedia Bratislava	4-0	0-5*	4-5	
1996/97	UEFA	Q2	FC Kosice	1-0	0-0*	1-0	
1963/64	CWC	QF	Slovan Bratislava	1-0*	1-0	2-0	
TOTAL				*6-0*	*1-5*	*7-5*	

SPAIN

Season	Comp	Stage	Opposition	H	A	Agg	Notes
2011/12	Europa	GS	Atletico Madrid	0-1	0-2*	0-3	
2008/09	EC	GS	Villarreal	2-0	0-1*	2-1	
2007/08	EC	GS	Barcelona	2-3*	0-1	2-4	
2004/05	EC	R1	Barcelona	1-3*	1-1	2-4	
2003/04	UEFA	QF	Villarreal	1-1*	0-2	1-3	
							Following EC elimination
2003/04	UEFA	R4	Barcelona	1-0*	0-0	1-0	
2002/03	UEFA	R3	Celta Vigo	1-0*	1-2	2-2	
						Following EC elimination, through on away goals	
2001/02	UEFA	R3	Valencia	1-0	0-1*	1-1	
						Lost 5-4 on penalties, following EC elimination	
1985/86	CWC	R1	Atletico Madrid	1-2	1-1*	2-3	
1982/83	EC	R2	Real Sociedad	2-1	0-2*	2-3	
1979/80	EC	QF	Real Madrid	2-0*	0-3	2-3	
1973/74	EC	SF	Atletico Madrid	0-0*	0-2	0-2	
1964/65	UEFA	R2	Barcelona	0-0	1-3*	1-3	
1962/63	UEFA	R1	Valencia	2-2	2-4*	4-6	
TOTAL				*16-13*	*6-25*	*22-38*	

SWITZERLAND

Season	Comp	Stage	Opposition	H	A	Agg	Notes
2011/12	Europa	PO	FC Sion	0-0*	1-3	1-3	*FC Sion expelled*
2002/03	EC	Q3	FC Basel	3-1*	0-2	3-3	*Lost on away goals*
1998/99	UEFA	R2	FC Zurich	1-1*	2-4	3-5	*Following EC elimination*
1993/94	UEFA	R1	Young Boys Berne	1-0	0-0*	1-0	
1991/92	UEFA	R2	Neuchatel Xamax	1-0	1-5*	2-5	
1973/74	EC	QF	FC Basel	4-2	2-3*	6-5	
1969/70	EC	R1	FC Basel	2-0	0-0*	2-0	
1966/67	EC	R1	FC Zurich	2-0*	3-0	5-0	
1963/64	CWC	R1	FC Basel	5-0	5-1*	10-1	
TOTAL				**19-4**	**14-18**	**33-22**	

UKRAINE

Season	Comp	Stage	Opposition	H	A	Agg	Notes
2007/08	EC	GS	Shakhtar Donetsk	2-1	0-2*	2-3	
2004/05	EC	R1	Shakhtar Donetsk	1-0	0-3*	1-3	
1986/87	EC	R2	Dinamo Kiev	1-1*	1-3	2-4	
1967/68	EC	R1	Dinamo Kiev	1-2*	1-1	2-3	
1965/66	CWC	QF	Dinamo Kiev	3-0*	1-1	4-1	
TOTAL				**8-4**	**3-10**	**11-14**	

WALES

Season	Comp	Stage	Opposition	H	A	Agg	Notes
1999/00	UEFA	Q1	Cwmbran Town	4-0	6-0*	10-0	
1997/98	UEFA	Q1	Inter Cardiff	5-0	3-0*	8-0	
TOTAL				**9-0**	**9-0**	**18-0**	

YUGOSLAVIA

Season	Comp	Stage	Opposition	H	A	Agg	Notes
1989/90	CWC	R1	Partizan Belgrade	5-4	1-2*	6-6	*Lost on away goals*
1968/69	EC	R2	Red Star Belgrade	5-1*	1-1	6-2	
1966/67	EC	QF	Vojvodina Novi Sad	2-0	0-1*	2-1	
TOTAL				**12-5**	**2-4**	**14-9**	

Aiden McGeady rejoices after giving the Hoops the lead against Villarreal in 2008

FIRST AND LAST - EUROPE

The first and last European games in the Hoops of four Celtic legends…

JOHN CLARK

First
Celtic 2-2 Valencia
24/10/62

JOHN CLARK'S European bow was in Celtic's very first European tie at Celtic Park as a 45,000 crowd saw the Hoops take on Valencia in the Inter-Cities Fairs Cup, the forerunner of the UEFA Cup and Europa League. The Celts had lost 4-2 in the first leg the previous month with Bobby Carroll scoring the club's first ever European goal and Paddy Crerand then being the first Hoop to score in Europe at Celtic Park. Amazingly, Clark and Stevie Chalmers were the only Lisbon Lions on the park that night.

Last
Celtic 3-0 Benfica
12/11/69

THERE had been a slight tilt in the balance over the intervening years and Celtic were now European giants and John Clark's final continental outing was against another European Cup-winning colossus in the shape of Benfica. An 80,000 crowd roared the Celts on against the Portuguese and the Hoops ran out 3-0 winners. The score was reversed in Lisbon but the Celts went through to the next round thanks to the toss of a coin!

WILLIE WALLACE

First
12/04/67
Celtic 3-1 Dukla Prague

ALTHOUGH he had signed in December 1966, Willie Wallace wasn't used in the March quarter-finals of the European Cup but made his debut against Dukla Prague in the semi-final first leg. And it was with the game finely balanced at 1-1, that two goals from Wallace inside six minutes gave the Hoops the 3-1 lead that would serve them until the final whistle was blown at the second-leg in Prague a fortnight later. Celtic, of course, won the European Cup that year with a 2-1 win over Inter Milan in Lisbon.

Last
Celtic 3-0 BK 1903 Copenhagen
29/09/71

CELTIC were shocked with a 2-1 first-leg defeat over in Denmark but a 53,000 crowd at Celtic Park saw Willie Wallace level the tie on aggregate and, after Tommy Callaghan had also scored, Wallace added another to give Celtic a 4-2 win over both legs. The Lisbon Lion had started his European chapter in the Hoops with two goals and he bowed out in the exact same fashion.

TOMMY BURNS

First
15/09/76
Celtic 2-2 Wisla Krakow

THE future Celtic manager was 19-years-old when he took his European bow and although Roddy MacDonald gave Celtic a 13th-minute lead in this UEFA Cup first-round, first-leg tie, two goals gave the Polish side a lead that wasn't curtailed until Kenny Dalglish scored the equaliser in the 90th minute. The Celts lost the away tie 2-0 but young Burns was to go on and have many European adventures with Celtic.

Last
Partizan Belgrade 2-1 Celtic
12/09/89

THE European Cup-Winners' Cup of season 1989/90 paired Celtic with the Yugoslavian side, and, although the Hoops lost 2-1 in Mostar, there was realistic hope that Mike Galloway's away goal would prove to be invaluable. Tommy Burns was a spectator for the return leg – one of the most amazing games ever seen at Celtic Park. Despite Celtic winning 5-4 with Jacki Dziekanowski scoring four, the tie finished 6-6 on aggregate and the Hoops went out on away goals.

HENRIK LARSSON

First
FC Tirol Innsbruck 2-1 Celtic
12/08/97

A GOAL in Austria from the unlikely source of Alan Stubbs gave Celtic hope in this UEFA Cup second qualifying round, first-leg which was the great Henrik Larsson's European debut for the Hoops. The 6-3 win at Celtic Park which saw Celtic win 7-5 on aggregate featured Henrik Larsson's first ever goal at Celtic Park – but unfortunately it was for the opposition as he put them 4-3 ahead on aggregate just before the break. With three minutes to go it was still 5-5 on aggregate and Celtic were out on away goals - until the two late strikes took them through.

Last
Villarreal 2-0 Celtic
14/04/04

THE Swede had scored Celtic's goal in the quarter-final first-leg as the Hoops drew 1-1 but hopes of reaching a second successive UEFA Cup final were dashed in this second leg with the Spanish side winning 2-0 in the Madrigal to take the tie 3-1 on aggregate. His strike was the last of 35 goals in 58 European games for the Hoops – the highest tally of any Celtic player.

CELTIC'S EUROPEAN RESULTS
SEASON BY SEASON

Season 1962/63:
Inter-Cities Fairs Cup
First round, 1st Leg: Valencia 4-2 Celtic
2nd Leg: Celtic 2-2 Valencia

Season 1963/64:
European Cup-Winners' Cup
First Round, 1st Leg: FC Basel 1-5 Celtic
2nd Leg: Celtic 5-0 FC Basel
Second Round, 1st Leg:
Celtic 3-0 Dinamo Zagreb
2nd Leg: Dinamo Zagreb 2-1 Celtic
Quarter-final, 1st Leg:
Celtic 1-0 Slovan Bratislava
2nd Leg: Slovan Bratislava 0-1 Celtic
Semi-final, 1st Leg:
Celtic 3-0 MTK Budapest
2nd Leg: MTK Budapest 4-0 Celtic

Season 1964/65:
Inter-Cities Fairs Cup
First Round, 1st Leg: Leixoes 1-1 Celtic
2nd Leg: Celtic 3-0 Leixoes
Second Round, 1st Leg:
Barcelona 3-1 Celtic
2nd Leg: Celtic 0-0 Barcelona

Season 1965/66:
European Cup-Winners' Cup
First Round, 1st Leg:
Go Ahead Deventer 0-6 Celtic
2nd Leg: Celtic 1-0 Go Ahead Deventer
Second Round, 1st Leg:
Aarhus GF 0-1 Celtic
2nd Leg: Celtic 2-0 Aarhus GF
Quarter-final, 1st Leg:
Celtic 3-0 Dinamo Kiev
2nd Leg: Dinamo Kiev 1-1 Celtic

Semi-final, 1st Leg: Celtic 1-0 Liverpool
2nd Leg: Liverpool 2-0 Celtic

Season 1966/67: European Cup
First Round, 1st Leg: Celtic 2-0 FC Zurich
2nd Leg: FC Zurich 0-3 Celtic
Second Round, 1st Leg:
FC Nantes 1-3 Celtic
2nd Leg: Celtic 3-1 FC Nantes
Quarter-final, 1st Leg:
Vojvodina Novi Sad 1-0 Celtic
2nd Leg: Celtic 2-0 Vojvodina Novi Sad
Semi-final, 1st Leg:
Celtic 3-1 Dukla Prague
2nd Leg: Dukla Prague 0-0 Celtic
Final: Celtic 2-1 Inter Milan

Season 1967/68: European Cup
First Round, 1st Leg:
Celtic 1-2 Dinamo Kiev
2nd Leg: Dinamo Kiev 1-1 Celtic

Season 1968/69: European Cup
First Round, 1st Leg: St Etienne 2-0 Celtic
2nd Leg: Celtic 4-0 St Etienne
Second Round, 1st Leg:
Celtic 5-1 Red Star Belgrade
2nd Leg: Red Star Belgrade 1-1 Celtic
Quarter-final, 1st Leg: AC Milan 0-0 Celtic
2nd Leg: Celtic 0-1 AC Milan

Season 1969/70: European Cup
First Round, 1st Leg: FC Basel 0-0 Celtic
2nd Leg: Celtic 2-0 FC Basel
Second Round, 1st Leg: Celtic 3-0 Benfica
2nd Leg: Benfica 3-0 Celtic
(Celtic won on Toss of Coin)
Quarter-final, 1st Leg: Celtic 3-0 Fiorentina

2nd Leg: Fiorentina 1-0 Celtic
Semi-final, 1st Leg: Leeds United 0-1 Celtic
2nd Leg: Celtic 2-1 Leeds United
Final: Celtic 1-2 Feyenoord

Season 1970/71: European Cup

First Round, 1st Leg: Celtic 9-0 KPV Kokkola
2nd Leg: KPV Kokkola 0-5 Celtic
Second Round, 1st Leg:
Waterford 0-7 Celtic
2nd Leg: Celtic 3-2 Waterford
Quarter-final, 1st Leg: Ajax 3-0 Celtic
2nd Leg: Celtic 1-0 Ajax

Season 1971/72: European Cup

First Round, 1st Leg:
B 1903 Copenhagen 1-2 Celtic
2nd Leg: Celtic 3-0 B 1903 Copenhagen 0
Second Round, 1st Leg: Celtic 5-0
Sliema Wanderers
2nd Leg: Sliema Wanderers 1-2 Celtic
Quarter-final, 1st Leg:
Ujpest Dozsa 1-2 Celtic
2nd Leg: Celtic 1-1 Ujpest Dozsa
Semi-final, 1st Leg: Inter Milan 0-0 Celtic
2nd Leg: Celtic 0-0 Inter Milan 0
(Inter Milan won 5-4 on penalties)

Season 1972/73: European Cup

First Round 1, 1st Leg:
Celtic 2-1 Rosenborg
2nd Leg: Rosenborg 1-3 Celtic
Second Round, 1st Leg:
Celtic 2-1 Ujpest Dozsa
2nd Leg: Ujpest Dozsa 3-0 Celtic

Season 1973/74: European Cup

First Round, 1st Leg: TPS Turku 1-6 Celtic
2nd Leg: Celtic 3-0 TPS Turku
Second Round, 1st Leg: Celtic 0-0 Vejle
2nd Leg: Vejle 0-1 Celtic
Quarter-final, 1st Leg: FC Basel 3-2 Celtic

2nd Leg: Celtic 4-2 FC Basel
Semi-final, 1st Leg:
Celtic 0-0 Atletico Madrid
2nd Leg: Atletico Madrid 2-0 Celtic

Season 1974/75: European Cup

First Round, 1st Leg:
Celtic 1-1 Olympiakos Piraeus
2nd Leg: Olympiakos Piraeus 2-0 Celtic

Season 1975/76:
European Cup-Winners' Cup

First Round 1, 1st Leg: Valur 0-2 Celtic
2nd Leg: Celtic 7-0 Valur
Second Round, 1st Leg: Boavista 0-0 Celtic
2nd Leg: Celtic 3-1 Boavista
Quarter-final, 1st Leg:
Celtic 1-1 Sachsenring Zwickau
2nd Leg: Sachsenring Zwickau 1-0 Celtic

Season 1976/77: UEFA Cup

First Round, 1st Leg:
Celtic 2-2 Wisla Krakow
2nd Leg: Wisla Krakow 2-0 Celtic

Season 1977/78: European Cup

First Round, 1st Leg:
Celtic 5-0 Jeunesse d'Esch
2nd Leg: Jeunesse d'Esch 1-6 Celtic
Second Round, 1st Leg:
Celtic 2-1 SWW Innsbruck
2nd Leg: SWW Innsbruck 3-0 Celtic

Season 1979/80: European Cup

First Round, 1st Leg:
Partizan Tirana 1-0 Celtic
2nd Leg: Celtic 4-1 Partizan Tirana
Second Round, 1st Leg: Celtic 3-2 Dundalk
2nd Leg: Dundalk 0-0 Celtic
Quarter-final, 1st Leg:
Celtic 2-0 Real Madrid
2nd Leg: Real Madrid 3-0 Celtic

Season 1980/81: European Cup-Winners' Cup

Preliminary Round, 1st Leg:
Celtic 6-0 Diosgyori Miskolc
2nd Leg: Diosgyori Miskolc 2-1 Celtic
First Round, 1st Leg:
Celtic 2-1 Politehnica Timisoara
2nd Leg: Politehnica Timisoara 1-0 Celtic
(Politehnica Timisoara won on the away goals rule)

Season 1981/82: European Cup

First Round, 1st Leg: Celtic 1-0 Juventus
2nd Leg: Juventus 2-0 Celtic

Season 1982/83: European Cup

First Round 1, 1st Leg: Celtic 2-2 Ajax
2nd Leg: Ajax 1-2 Celtic
Second Round, 1st Leg:
Real Sociedad 2-0 Celtic
2nd Leg: Celtic 2-1 Real Sociedad

Season 1983/84: UEFA Cup

First Round, 1st Leg: Celtic 1-0 Aarhus GF
2nd Leg: Aarhus GF 1-4 Celtic
Second Round, 1st Leg:
Sporting Lisbon 2-0 Celtic
2nd Leg: Celtic 5-0 Sporting Lisbon
Third Round, 1st Leg:
Nottingham Forest 0-0 Celtic
2nd Leg: Celtic 1-2 Nottingham Forest

Tommy Burns (centre) celebrates his goal against Sporting Lisbon with Paul McStay and Murdo MacLeod

Season 1984/85: European Cup-Winners' Cup

First Round, 1st Leg: KAA Gent 0-1 Celtic
2nd Leg: Celtic 3-0 KAA Gent
Second Round, 1st Leg:
Rapid Vienna 3-1 Celtic
2nd Leg: Celtic 0-1 Rapid Vienna
(Played at Old Trafford)

Season 1985/86: European Cup-Winners' Cup

First Round, 1st Leg:
Atletico Madrid 1-1 Celtic
2nd Leg: Celtic 1-2 Atletico Madrid

Season 1986/87: European Cup

First Round, 1st Leg:
Shamrock Rovers 0-1 Celtic
2nd Leg: Celtic 2-0 Shamrock Rovers
Second Round, 1st Leg:
Celtic 1-1 Dinamo Kiev
2nd Leg: Dinamo Kiev 3-1 Celtic

Season 1987/88: UEFA Cup

First Round, 1st Leg: Celtic 2-1
Borussia Dortmund
2nd Leg: Borussia Dortmund 2-0 Celtic

Season 1988/89: European Cup

First Round, 1st Leg: Honved 1-0 Celtic
2nd Leg: Celtic 4-0 Honved
Second Round, 1st Leg:
Celtic 0-1 Werder Bremen
2nd Leg: Werder Bremen 0-0 Celtic

Season 1989/90: European Cup-Winners' Cup

First Round, 1st Leg:
Partizan Belgrade 2-1 Celtic
2nd Leg: Celtic 5-4 Partizan Belgrade
(Partizan Belgrade won on the away goals rule)

Season 1991/92: UEFA Cup

First Round, 1st Leg:
Celtic 2-0 Germinal Ekeren
2nd Leg: Germinal Ekeren 1-1 Celtic
Second Round, 1st Leg:
Neuchatal Xamax 5-1 Celtic
2nd Leg: Celtic 1-0 Neuchatal Xamax

Season 1992/93: UEFA Cup

First Round, 1st Leg: FC Cologne 2-0 Celtic
2nd Leg: Celtic 3-0 FC Cologne
Second Round, 1st Leg:
Borussia Dortmund 1-0 Celtic
2nd Leg: Celtic 1-2 Borussia Dortmund

Season 1993/94: UEFA Cup

First Round, 1st Leg:
BSC Young Boys 0-0 Celtic
2nd Leg: Celtic 1-0 BSC Young Boys
Second Round, 1st Leg:
Celtic 1-0 Sporting Lisbon
2nd Leg: Sporting Lisbon 2-0 Celtic

Season 1995/96:
European Cup-Winners' Cup

First Round, 1st Leg:
Dinamo Batumi 2-3 Celtic
2nd Leg: Celtic 4-0 Dinamo Batumi
Second Round, 1st Leg:
Paris St Germain 1-0 Celtic
2nd Leg: Celtic 0-3 Paris St Germain

Season 1996/97: UEFA Cup

Qualifying Round, 1st Leg:
FC Kosice 0-0 Celtic
2nd Leg: Celtic 1-0 FC Kosice
First Round, 1st Leg:
Celtic 0-2 Hamburg SV
2nd Leg: Hamburg SV 2-0 Celtic

Season 1997/98: UEFA Cup

First Qualifying Round, 1st Leg:

Inter Cabel-Tel 0-3 Celtic
2nd Leg: Celtic 5-0 Inter Cabel-Tel
Second Qualifying Round, 1st Leg:
FC Tirol Innsbruck 2-1 Celtic
2nd Leg: Celtic 6-3 FC Tirol Innsbruck
First Round, 1st Leg: Celtic 2-2 Liverpool
2nd Leg: Liverpool 0-0 Celtic
(Liverpool won on the away goals rule)

Season 1998/99:
UEFA Champions League

First Qualifying Round, 1st Leg:
Celtic 0-0 St Patrick's Athletic
2nd Leg: St Patrick's Athletic 0-2 Celtic
Second Qualifying Round, 1st Leg:
Celtic 1-0 Croatia Zagreb
2nd Leg: Croatia Zagreb 3-0 Celtic
UEFA Cup
First Round, 1st Leg:
Vitoria Guimaraes 1-2 Celtic
2nd Leg: Celtic 2-1 Vitoria Guimaraes
Second Round, 1st Leg:
Celtic 1-1 FC Zurich
2nd Leg: FC Zurich 4-2 Celtic

Season 1999/2000: UEFA Cup

Qualifying Round, 1st Leg:
Cwmbran Town 0-6 Celtic
2nd Leg: Celtic 4-0 Cwmbran Town
First Round, 1st Leg:
Celtic 2-0 Hapoel Tel Aviv
2nd Leg: Hapoel Tel Aviv 0-1 Celtic
Second Round, 1st Leg:
Olympique Lyon 1-0 Celtic
2nd Leg: Celtic 0-1 Olympique Lyon

Season 2000/01: UEFA Cup

Qualifying Round, 1st Leg:
Jeunesse d'Esch 0-4 Celtic
2nd Leg: Celtic 7-0 Jeunesse d'Esch
First Round, 1st Leg:
Celtic 2-0 HJK Helsinki

2nd Leg: HJK Helsinki 2-1 Celtic
Second Round, 1st Leg:
Bordeaux 1-1 Celtic
2nd Leg: Celtic 1-2 Bordeaux

Season 2001/02:
UEFA Champions League

Third Qualifying Round, 1st Leg:
Ajax 1-3 Celtic
2nd Leg: Celtic 0-1 Ajax
Group Stage:
Juventus 3-2 Celtic
Celtic 1-0 FC Porto
Celtic 1-0 Rosenborg
FC Porto 3-0 Celtic
Rosenborg 2-0 Celtic
Celtic 4-3 Juventus 3

UEFA Cup

Third Round, 1st Leg: Valencia 1-0 Celtic
2nd Leg: Celtic 1-0 Valencia
(Valencia won 5-4 on penalties)

Season 2002/03:
UEFA Champions League

Third Qualifying Round, 1st Leg:
Celtic 3-1 FC Basel
2nd Leg: FC Basel 2-0 Celtic
(FC Basel won on the away goals rule)

UEFA Cup

First Round, 1st Leg:
Celtic 8-1 FK Suduva
2nd Leg: FK Suduva 0-2 Celtic
Second Round, 1st Leg:
Celtic 1-0 Blackburn Rovers
2nd Leg: Blackburn Rovers 0-2 Celtic
Third Round, 1st Leg:
Celtic 1-0 Celta Vigo
2nd Leg: Celta Vigo 2 v Celtic 1
(Celtic won the away goals rule)
Fourth Round, 1st Leg:
Celtic 3-1 VfB Stuttgart
2nd Leg: VfB Stuttgart 3-2 Celtic

Quarter-final, 1st Leg:
Celtic 1-1 Liverpool
2nd Leg: Liverpool 0-2 Celtic
Semi-final, 1st Leg: Celtic 1-1 Boavista
2nd Leg: Boavista 0-1 Celtic
Final: Celtic 2-3 FC Porto

Season 2003/04:
UEFA Champions League

Second Qualifying Round: 1st Leg:
FBK Kaunas 0-4 Celtic
2nd Leg: Celtic 1-0 FBK Kaunas
Third Qualifying Round, 1st Leg:
MTK Hungaria 0-4 Celtic
2nd Leg: Celtic 1-0 MTK Hungaria
Group Stage:
Bayern Munich 2-1 Celtic
Celtic 2-0 Olympique Lyon
Anderlecht 1-0 Celtic
Celtic 3-1 Anderlecht
Celtic 0-0 Bayern Munich
Olympique Lyon 3-2 Celtic

UEFA Cup

Third Round, 1st Leg:
Celtic 3-0 FK Teplice
2nd Leg: FK Teplice 1-0 Celtic
Fourth Round, 1st Leg:
Celtic 1-0 Barcelona
2nd Leg: Barcelona 0-0 Celtic
Quarter-final, 1st Leg:
Celtic 1-1 Villarreal
2nd Leg: Villarreal 2-0 Celtic

Season 2004/05:
UEFA Champions League

Group Stage:
Celtic 1-3 Barcelona
AC Milan 3-1 Celtic
Shakhtar Donetsk 3-0 Celtic
Celtic 1-0 Shakhtar Donetsk
Barcelona 1-1 Celtic
Celtic 0-0 AC Milan

Season 2005/06:
UEFA Champions League
Second Qualifying Round, 1st Leg:
Artmedia Bratislava 5-0 Celtic
2nd Leg: Celtic 4-0 Artmedia Bratislava

Season 2006/07:
UEFA Champions League
Group Stage"
Manchester United 3-2 Celtic
Celtic 1-0 FC Copenhagen
Celtic 3-0 Benfica
Benfica 3-0 Celtic
Celtic 1-0 Manchester United
FC Copenhagen 3-1 Celtic
First Knock-Out Round, 1st Leg:
Celtic 0-0 AC Milan
2nd Leg: AC Milan 1-0 Celtic

Season 2007/08:
UEFA Champions League
Third Qualifying Round, 1st Leg:
Spartak Moscow 1-1 Celtic
2nd Leg: Celtic 1-1 Spartak Moscow
(Celtic won 4-3 on penalties)
Group Stage:
Shakhtar Donetsk 2-0 Celtic
Celtic 2-1 AC Milan
Benfica 1-0 Celtic
Celtic 1-0 Benfica
Celtic 2-1 Shakhtar Donetsk
AC Milan 1-0 Celtic
First Knock-Out Round, 1st Leg:
Celtic 2-3 Barcelona
2nd Leg: Barcelona 1-0 Celtic

Season 2008/09:
UEFA Champions League
Group Stage:
Celtic 0-0 Aalborg BK
Villarreal 1-0 Celtic
Manchester United 3-0 Celtic

Celtic 1-1 Manchester United
Aalborg BK 2-1 Celtic
Celtic 2-0 Villarreal

Season 2009/10:
UEFA Champions League
Third Qualifying Round, 1st Leg:
Celtic 0-1 Dinamo Moscow
2nd Leg: Dinamo Moscow 0-2 Celtic
Fourth Qualifying Round, 1st Leg:
Celtic 0-2 Arsenal
2nd Leg: Arsenal 3-1 Celtic
UEFA Europa League
Group Stage:
Hapoel Tel Aviv 2-1 Celtic
Celtic 1-1 Rapid Vienna
Celtic 0-1 Hamburg SV
Hamburg SV 0-0 Celtic
Celtic 2-0 Hapoel Tel Aviv
Rapid Vienna 3-3 Celtic

Season 2010/11:
UEFA Champions League
Third Qualifying Round, 1st Leg:
Braga 3-0 Celtic
2nd Leg: Celtic 2-1 Braga
UEFA Europa League
Play-Off Round, 1st Leg:
Celtic 2-0 FC Utrecht
2nd Leg: FC Utrecht 4-0 Celtic

Season 2011/12:
UEFA Europa League
Play-Off Round, 1st Leg: Celtic 0-0 FC Sion
2nd Leg: FC Sion 3-1 Celtic (Sion expelled)
Group Stage:
Atletico Madrid 2-0 Celtic
Celtic 1-1 Udinese
Rennes 1-1 Celtic
Celtic 3-1 Rennes
Celtic 0-1 Atletico Madrid
Udinese 1-1 Celtic

EUROPEAN CUP WINNERS

1956
Real Madrid 4-3 Rheims
1957
Real Madrid 2-0 Fiorentina
1958
Real Madrid 3-2 AC Milan
1959
Real Madrid 2-0 Rheims
1960
Real Madrid 7-3 Eintracht Frankfurt
1961
Benfica 3-2 Barcelona
1962
Benfica 5-3 Real Madrid
1963
AC Milan 2-1 Benfica
1964
Inter Milan 3-1 Real Madrid
1965
Inter Milan 1-0 Benfica
1966
Real Madrid 2-1 Partizan Belgrade
1967
Celtic 2-1 Inter Milan
1968
Manchester United 4-1 Benfica
1969
AC Milan 4-1 Ajax
1970
Feyenoord 2-1 Celtic
1971
Ajax 2-0 Panathinaikos
1972
Ajax 2-0 Inter Milan
1973
Ajax 1-0 Juventus
1974
Bayern Munich 1-1 Atletico Madrid
(R) Bayern Mun 4-1 Atletico Mad

1975
Bayern Munich 2-0 Leeds United
1976
Bayern Munich 1-0 St Etienne
1977
Liverpool 3-1 Borussia
Moenchengladbach
1978
Liverpool 1-0 FC Bruges
1979
Nottingham Forest 1-0 Malmo
1980
Nottingham Forest 1-0 SV Hamburg
1981
Liverpool 1-0 Real Madrid
1982
Aston Villa 1-0 Bayern Munich
1983
SV Hamburg 1-0 Juventus
1984
Liverpool 1-1 Roma
(Liverpool win on penalties)
1985
Juventus 1-0 Liverpool
1986
Steaua Bucharest 0-0 Barcelona
(Steaua Bucharest win on penalties)
1987
FC Porto 2-1 Bayern Munich
1988
PSV Eindhoven 0-0 Benfica
(PSV win on penalties)
1989
AC Milan 4-0 Steaua Bucharest
1990
AC Milan 1-0 Benfica
1991
Red Star Belgrade 0-0 Marseille
(Red Star win on penalties)

1992
Barcelona 1-0 Sampdoria
1993
Marseille 1-0 AC Milan
1994
AC Milan 4-0 Barcelona
1995
Ajax 1-0 AC Milan
1996
Juventus 1-1 Ajax
(Juventus win on penalties)
1997
Borussia Dortmund 3-1 Juventus
1998
Real Madrid 1-0 Juventus
1999
Manchester Utd 2-1 Bayern Munich
2000
Real Madrid 3-0 Valencia
2001
Bayern Munich 1-1 Valencia
(Bayern Munich win on penalties)
2002
Real Madrid 2-1 Bayer Leverkusen

2003
AC Milan 0-0 Juventus
(AC Milan win on penalties)
2004
FC Porto 3-0 AS Monaco
2005
Liverpool 3-3 AC Milan
(Liverpool win on penalties)
2006
Barcelona 2-1 Arsenal
2007
AC Milan 2-1 Liverpool
2008
Manchester United 1-1 Chelsea
(Manchester win on penalties)
2009
Barcelona 2-0 Manchester United
2010
Inter Milan 2-0 Bayern Munich
2011
Barcelona 3-1 Manchester United
2012
Chelsea 1-1 Bayern Munich
(Chelsea win on penalties)

The Lisbon Lions

UEFA CUP WINNERS (Fairs' Cities Cup 1958-71)

1958
Barcelona 8-2 London
1960
Barcelona 5-2 Birmingham City
1961
Roma 4-2 Birmingham City
1962
Valencia 7-3 Barcelona
1963
Valencia 4-1 Dinamo Zagreb
1964
Real Zaragoza 2-1 Valencia
1965
Ferencvaros 1-0 Juventus
1966
Barcelona 4-3 Real Zaragoza
1967
Dinamo Zagreb 2-0 Leeds United
1968
Leeds United 1-0 Ferencvaros
1969
Newcastle Utd 6-2 Ujpest Dozsa
1970
Arsenal 4-3 Anderlecht
1971
Juventus 3-3 Leeds United
(Leeds United win on away goals)
1972
Tottenham Hotspur 3-2 Wolves
1973
Liverpool 3-2 Borussia
Moenchengladbach
1974
Feyenoord 4-2 Tottenham Hotspur
1975
Borussia Moenchengladbach 5-1
FC Twente
1976
Liverpool 4-3 FC Brugge

1977
Juventus 2-2 Athletic Bilbao
(Juventus win on away goals)
1978
PSV Eindhoven 3-0 Bastia
1979
Borussia Moenchengladbach 2-1
Red Star Belgrade
1980
Eintracht Frankfurt 3-3 Borussia
Moenchengladbach
(Eintracht win on away goals)
1981
Ipswich Town 5-4 AZ '67
1982
IFK Gothenburg 4-0 SV Hamburg
1983
Anderlecht 2-1 Benfica
1984
Tottenham Hotspur 2-2 Anderlecht
(Tottenham win on penalties)
1985
Real Madrid 3-1 Videoton
1986
Real Madrid 5-3 Cologne
1987
IFK Gothenburg 2-1 Dundee United
1988
Bayer Leverkusen 3-3 Espanyol
(B Leverkusen win on penalties)
1989
Napoli 5-4 VfB Stuttgart
1990
Juventus 3-1 Fiorentina
1991
Inter Milan 2-1 Roma
1992
Ajax 2-2 Torino
(Ajax win on away goals)

1993
Juventus 6-1 Borussia Dortmund
1994
Inter Milan 2-0 Austria Salzburg
1995
Parma 2-1 Juventus
1996
Bayern Munich 5-1 Bordeaux
1997
Schalke '04 1-1 Inter Milan
(Schalke win on penalties)
1998
Inter Milan 3-0 Lazio
1999
Parma 3-0 Marseille
2000
Galatasaray 0-0 Arsenal
(Galatasaray win on penalties)
2001
Liverpool 5-4 Alaves
2002
Feyenoord 3-2 Borussia Dortmund
2003
FC Porto 3-2 Celtic

2004
Valencia 2-0 Marseille
2005
CSKA Moscow 3-1 Sporting Lisbon
2006
Sevilla 4-0 Middlesbrough
2007
Sevilla 2-2 Espanyol
(Sevilla win on penalties)
2008
Zenit St Petersburg 2-0 Rangers
2009
Shakhtar Donetsk 2-1
Werder Bremen
2010
Atletico Madrid 2-1 Fulham
2011
FC Porto 1-0 SC Braga
2012
Atletico Madrid 3-0
Athletic Bilbao

• Final over two legs until 1998
(with exception of 1964 & '65)

Anthony Stokes levels in the Hoops' 3-1 Europa League victory over Rennes in 2011

EUROPEAN CUP-WINNERS' CUP WINNERS

1961*
Fiorentina 4-1 Rangers
1962*
Atletico Madrid 4-1 Fiorentina
1963
Tottenham 5-1 Atletico Madrid
1964
Sporting Lisbon 3-3 MTK Budapest
(R) Sp. Lisbon 1-0 MTK Budapest
1965
West Ham Utd 2-0 1860 Munich
1966
Borussia Dortmund 2-1 Liverpool
1967
Bayern Munich 1-0 Rangers
1968
AC Milan 2-0 SV Hamburg

1969
Slovan Bratislava 3-2 Barcelona
1970
Man City 2-1 Gornik Zabrze
1971
Chelsea 1-1 Real Madrid
(R) Chelsea 2-1 Real Madrid
1972
Rangers 3-2 Dynamo Moscow
1973
AC Milan 1-0 Leeds United
1974
AC Magdeburg 2-0 AC Milan
1975
Dynamo Kiev 3-0 Ferencvaros
1976
Anderlecht 4-2 West Ham United

Roy Aitken and Tom McAdam double up in the 3-0 'win' over Rapid Vienna in 1984

1977
SV Hamburg 2-0 Anderlecht
1978
Anderlecht 4-0 Austria Vienna
1979
Barcelona 4-3 Fortuna Dusseldorf
1980
Valencia 0-0 Arsenal
(Valencia win on penalties)
1981
Dynamo Tbilisi 2-1 Carl Zeiss Jena
1982
Barcelona 2-1 Standard Liège
1983
Aberdeen 2-1 Real Madrid
1984
Juventus 2-1 FC Porto
1985
Everton 3-1 Rapid Vienna
1986
Dynamo Kiev 3-0 Atletico Madrid
1987
Ajax 1-0 Lokomotiv Leipzig
1988
KV Mechelen 1-0 Ajax
1989
Barcelona 2-0 Sampdoria
1990
Sampdoria 2-0 Anderlecht
1991
Manchester United 2-1 Barcelona
1992
Werder Bremen 2-0 AS Monaco
1993
Parma 3-1 Antwerp
1994
Arsenal 1-0 Parma
1995
Real Zaragoza 2-1 Arsenal

1996
Paris St. Germain 1-0 Rapid Vienna
1997
Barcelona 1-0 Paris St. Germain
1998
Chelsea 1-0 VfB Stuttgart
1999
Lazio 2-1 Mallorca

* Final played over two legs

Mike Galloway jostles for possession during the famous 5-4 game against Partizan Belgrade in 1989

CELTIC MANAGERS

Willie Maley (1897-1940)

Willie Maley was Celtic's first ever manager. A talented and influential half-back, he had been there from the very beginning, playing in the club's inaugural match, a 5-2 thumping of Rangers. After his playing career ended nine years later, he was appointed secretary-manager of the Hoops at the age of 29, taking over team duties which had been previously carried out by a committee. It was an astute decision. If Celtic's seeds had sprouted in the garden of Scottish football, Maley ensured they flourished into something colossal as he made the club one of the dominant forces in the domestic game. A shrewd spotter of talent, he remained in his post for a staggering 43 years, creating some of the finest Celtic teams to grace the field and guiding the team to an incredible 30 first-class trophies. That's a record unlikely to be ever matched.

Honours: League Championships (16), Scottish Cups (14)

Jimmy McStay (1940-45)

A devoted servant to Celtic, Jimmy McStay spent the best part of two decades with the Hoops as a dependable and inspirational defender, making over 400 appearances in the process. However, his tenure would be during the war years of 1940-45, a period when Scottish football suffered huge disruption. If that wasn't enough for McStay, he had to contend with increased boardroom interference, which he never managed to quell. Inevitably, the result was stagnation with little tangible success. It would be a recurring theme for the next 20 years.

Honours: None (as normal competitions were suspended during war-time)

Jimmy McGrory (1945-1965)

With his incredible goalscoring record, Jimmy McGrory was considered the greatest ever Celtic player before he took over the managerial reins from Jimmy McStay in 1945. But McGrory's success off the park didn't mirror his exploits on it. Sure, there were some triumphs – the Coronation Cup win in 1953, the League and Scottish Cup double in 1954 and the 7-1 humiliation of Rangers in the League Cup final at Hampden in 1957 are all momentous occasions in the club's history - but generally it was a period of massive under-achievement. This was mainly due to the continual meddling in team affairs by the board, which effectively relegated McGrory into a peripheral role. That situation would only change when Jock Stein took over.

Honours: The Coronation Cup (1) League Championship (1), Scottish Cup (2), League Cup (2)

Jock Stein (1965-1978)

Jock Stein was the greatest manager in Celtic's history, and one of the finest in the history of the game. A football visionary, his achievements at the club are the stuff of legend. In the space of two years, he transformed a side lacking direction and struggling to challenge for honours in Scotland into the best team in Europe, whilst playing an attractive, adventurous brand of football – all with players born within 30 miles of Glasgow. Along with that European Cup victory in Lisbon, notably, he also guided the Hoops to a record-breaking nine league championships in a row. It was a glorious reign of unparalleled success. There have been many Hoops heroes throughout the club's existence but Stein's name stands above all others. In March 2011, a statue of the great man holding the European Cup was unveiled at the entrance to Celtic Park. As Bill Shankly famously said to Stein in the aftermath of the Lisbon triumph: 'John, you're immortal now.'

Honours: European Cup (1), League Championship (10), Scottish Cup (8), League Cup (6)

Billy McNeill (1978-81) (1987-91)

When the time came to select a successor to the legendary figure of Jock Stein, his leader on the pitch, Billy McNeill, seemed the natural choice. Cesar, who had retired after a glorious career three years earlier, had already enjoyed shorts stints in charge at Clyde and Aberdeen. He swiftly brought success back to Paradise in his first season, with the league title delivered dramatically as the 10 men of Celtic beat Rangers 4-2 in their final fixture of the campaign. McNeill managed to win another four trophies, before taking over as Manchester City boss in 1983. He returned to the club he loved four years later, though, just in time for the fairytale centenary season as the Hoops claimed the league and cup double. Success would be in short supply after that, however, with Celtic unable to match Rangers' financial clout and McNeill departed the hot seat for the final time in 1991.

Honours: League Championship (4), Scottish Cup (3), League Cup (1)

Davie Hay (1983-87)

Davie Hay was only 35-years-old when he succeeded McNeill. With only a short but successful stint at Motherwell on his managerial CV, the Celtic great didn't have huge experience either. However, he set about his task with vigour and was extremely unfortunate not win at least one piece of silverware in his first season at the helm as the Hoops finished as runners-up in every competition. Trophies eventually arrived with the Scottish Cup victory in 1985 and the memorable last day League Championship triumph at Love Street in the following season. With players such as Paul McStay and Brian McClair, Hay had constructed a team with plenty of talent, particularly in the attacking department. However, after failing to land any prizes in his fourth campaign, he was dismissed. **Honours: League Championship (1) Scottish Cup (1)**

Liam Brady (1991-93)

Liam Brady became the first Celtic boss to take charge without having previously played for the club and his inexperience proved costly over his three seasons. It wasn't a good start for Brady who suffered one of the worst European defeats in the club's history, going down 5-1 to Swiss minnows Neuchatel Xamax. There was also a sloppy defeat on the final day of the season which saw the Hoops drop to third place in the league. He did bring Tom Boyd to the club in 1992, but Celtic failed to close the gap on Rangers or reach any cup finals. His third season did not bode any better and Brady became the first Hoops manager to tender his resignation entirely of his own volition. **Honours: None**

Lou Macari (1993-1994)

After many years of management in the English lower leagues, Lou Macari attempted to stamp a similar style of football on Celtic when he arrived in October 1993. He won his first Glasgow derby, 2-1, three days after his appointment, but results failed to remain positive. A 4-2 defeat at New Year to Rangers, after trailing 3-0 did nothing to boost morale during a difficult time in the club's history. Macari was in charge when the takeover occurred, but his relationship with new owner Fergus McCann did not last long. Just three months later he was dismissed. **Honours: None**

Tommy Burns (1994-1997)

Tommy Burns was more than just a footballer. He was also a manager and a coach during his lifetime, but more importantly he also personified everything good about Celtic Football Club. When he was appointed manager in 1995 it was during a period of domestic dominance by Rangers, but he began to restore pride at Celtic Park and got his team playing exciting and attractive football. Celtic won their first trophy for six years under him when they lifted the Scottish Cup in 1995, beating Airdrie 1-0 in the final. It was to be the only silverware Burns would lift as the Celtic manager, though, despite an outstanding second season in charge. The Hoops only lost one league game, but they still finished second. In 1997, after finishing second again, he was sacked by Fergus McCann. He would later return to the club he loved, however, and was first-team coach alongside as part of Gordon Strachan's coaching team when they won three league titles in a row. Sadly, Tommy Burns didn't live to see the third of those triumphs. He passed away on May 15, 2008 at the age of just 51. **Honours: Scottish Cup (1)**

Wim Jansen (1997-1998)

Few are likely to remember Wim Jansen's poor start to his managerial career at Celtic because of the success he went on to achieve. He was the man responsible for bringing Henrik Larsson to the club and won the club's first League Cup in 15 years, but even more importantly, he led Celtic to one of the most important titles in their history stopping Rangers' bid for 10-in-a-row. Celtic's League Cup success when they beat Dundee United 3-0 in the final, coupled with the 2-0 New Year derby victory, boosted the team's confidence. The campaign ended in glory for the Hoops as they beat St Johnstone 2-0 on the final day of the season, but Jansen stunned the club when he quit in the immediate aftermath of that triumph.

Honours: League Championship (1), League Cup (1)

Dr Jozef Venglos (1998-1999)

The arrival of 'Dr Jo' was a surprise, not only because the departure of Wim Jansen had been so unexpected, but because the Slovak was also a relatively unknown name. Failing to qualify for the UEFA Champions League and dropping out of the UEFA Cup put massive pressure on Venglos' shoulders, but a 5-1 thumping of Rangers in November gave him some much needed breathing space. With signings like Lubo Moravcik and Johan Mjallby beginning to show their worth, the fans got behind the manager and fortunes looked to be changing. But the damage had already been done at the start of the season and it was always going to be difficult to claw back the deficit. Their one remaining hope of success lay with the Scottish Cup but a disappointing performance in the final meant the Hoops ended the season with no silverware and Venglos eventually moved on. **Honours: None**

John Barnes (1999-2000)

Kenny Dalglish's 'Dream Team' didn't last as long as he had hoped. The Celtic legend took over as Director of Football and appointed the former England star John Barnes as manager. Hampered by the loss of Henrik Larsson who suffered a horrific leg break in the UEFA Cup, Celtic began to drop crucial points in the league. The third round Scottish Cup defeat at home to Inverness Caledonian Thistle killed off any hopes of Barnes turning Celtic's fortunes around and Barnes' was subsequently dismissed the following day. Dalglish assumed a caretaker manager role, and helped the club win the League Cup that season.

Honours: None

Martin O'Neill (2000-2005)

Celtic's most influential manager since Jock Stein announced his arrival in dramatic style when his side beat Rangers 6-2 in the first derby of the season.

O'Neill won the treble in his first season before retaining the league title the following season. He also steered the club to their first European final in 33 years when his side reached the UEFA Cup final in 2003, having seen off Liverpool en route to the final in Seville. Unfortunately, the adventure was to end with a 3-2 extra-time defeat against FC Porto. A further league title arrived the following season, and O'Neill finished his tenure with a Scottish Cup triumph, which was, unfortunately, overshadowed, by a final day league defeat at Fir Park which cost the title. He won 76 per cent of matches played during his five years in charge, but more importantly, installed pride and belief back into Paradise again.

Honours: League Championship (3), Scottish Cup (3), League Cup (1)

Gordon Strachan (2005-2009)

Gordon Strachan won three Championships, one Scottish Cup and two League Cups for Celtic and also took the club into the last 16 of the UEFA Champions League for the first time in their history, secured with a momentous 1-0 victory over Manchester United in 2007. His third title was an emotional one, coming just days after the sad and untimely death of Celtic legend, Tommy Burns, who was first-team coach at the team and also a friend of Strachan's. On the field, Strachan's Celtic team matched their European achievement on 2007 by reaching the last 16 of the Champions League the following year.

Honours: League Championship (3), Scottish Cup (1), League Cup (2)

Tony Mowbray (2009-2010)

After a successful spell at Hibernian and winning the English Championship with West Brom, Tony Mowbray was a popular choice to replace Gordon Strachan. However, it proved to be a less than successful tenure, as Celtic's challenge for trophies, in particular the league title, faltered. A 4-0 away defeat to St Mirren heralded the end of Mowbray's short reign as Celtic boss.

Honours: None

Neil Lennon (2010 – present day)

Neil Lennon stepped up from coach of Celtic's Development Squad to become caretaker manager in the aftermath of Tony Mowbray's departure, and although he couldn't prevent a disastrous Scottish Cup semi-final defeat to Ross County, Lennon's side won their last eight SPL fixtures, and the Irishman took over the manager's position on a permanent basis in June 2010. In his first season as boss, his newly-assembled side produced some scintillating football, and while they narrowly missed out on the league title and the League Cup, they lifted the Scottish Cup. Lennon took the side to greater heights in 2011/12 when they delivered the title in fine style after being 15 points behind at one point.

Honours: League Championship (1), Scottish Cup (1)

CELTIC'S
ACADEMY

CELTIC YOUTH SQUADS

UNDER-20s

COACHES:
John Kennedy, Tommy McIntrye

GLENN DANIELS

One of last summer's signings, Glenn Daniels, is from Belgium and made the move to the Hoops from Birmingham City. The teenager plays in goal and with Robbie Thomson moving up to the Development Squad, he will be fighting it out with Leo Fasan for a place between the sticks this season.

LEO FASAN

The Italian goalkeeper has worked his way through the youth levels at Celtic and won the Jack Wood Trophy in 2010 with the Under-16s. He's started two Glasgow Cup finals for the 17s, winning the trophy on his second attempt, and last season filled in well for the injured Robbie Thomson, for the 19s.

STUART FINDLAY

U17s' captain, Findlay, made his first-team debut in the testimonial match against Norwich City at the end of last season. He played the full 90 minutes and was outstanding in central defence alongside Kelvin Wilson. He has been at Celtic since U11 level and also has experience in the NextGen Series.

DENNY JOHNSTONE

Up front, Johnstone is a strong player who can hold the ball up well. But he also has pace on his side and a good range of goals in his tank. He has both NextGen Series and Glasgow Cup experience under his belt along with featuring for the 19s last season too.

LEWIS KIDD

The central midfielder has big boots to fill now Callum McGregor and Jackson Irvine are graduating from the Youth Academy. But he is a Scottish internationalist and featured for the first-team in the friendly against Norwich so already has the ability and experience to deal with the pressure.

JACK KIRWAN

The Scottish internationalist plays up front and scored for his country against England in the Victory Shield in 2011. He featured heavily for Celtic's 17s last season and was unlucky to suffer defeat in the Glasgow Cup final to Rangers, on penalties.

JAMIE LINDSAY

As another youth player to make his first-team debut against Norwich at the end of the season, Lindsay showed he had put his Glasgow Cup final penalty miss behind him. His shot cracked off the woodwork in the penalty shoot-out, but the midfielder has enough talent to move on from that memory.

PADDY McNALLY

The centre-half from Belfast signed at the start of the 2010/11 season but was left frustrated when his registration was delayed. That ruled him out of competitive action for a few months, so he will be desperate to make an impact right from the start of the 2012/13 campaign.

MICHAEL MILLER

After leaving school and winning the Glasgow Cup at the end of the 2010/11 season, Miller's performances left the coaches no choice but to push him into the 19s' side. Despite being one of the youngest in the team, the right-back showed great composure and maturity throughout the campaign.

UNDER-17s

THE cruel lottery of a penalty shoot-out stopped Celtic Under-17s from getting their hands on silverware this season – but ultimately it was still a successful season for Miodrag Krivokapic's youngsters.

There is just one trophy up for grabs at U17 level in Scotland – the historic Glasgow Cup, formerly contested by senior teams until the late 1980s. Having won the competition the previous season thanks to Paul George's goal, the young Hoops had high hopes of retaining their crown after reaching the final again this year where they faced Rangers at Ibrox.

After passing up several excellent opportunities, they deservedly opened the scoring through Paul McLellan in the second half. However, Darren Ramsey levelled for the hosts three minutes later, and with both teams unable to fashion a winner before the end of normal time the match was settled from 12 yards. And it was the Ibrox side who came out on top, winning the shootout 4-2 to lift the cup and leave the young Celts disappointed.

Nevertheless, the Bhoys could be proud of the way they performed on the big stage, and there were plenty other reasons for encouragement this season. While winning silverware is always an aim of the Celtic Youth Academy, the overriding objective is developing players for the first team. And towards the end of May, five individuals from the U17s made their bow for Neil Lennon's side in

Celtic U17s show their team spirit ahead of the 2012 Glasgow Cup final penalty shoot-out

Stuart Findlay (below) and Lewis Kidd (bottom) were among several U17 players to make a first-team appearance in Adam Drury's testimonial

Adam Drury's Testimonial against Norwich City.

Captain, Stuart Findlay, was named in the starting XI at Carrow Road and he lined up against the formidable figure of leading Premier League marksman, Grant Holt.

In the second half, Lewis Kidd, Paddy McNally, Denny Johnstone and Jamie Lindsay also entered the fray from the bench to make their debuts.

They all acquitted themselves well against top-quality opposition, particularly Findlay, who played the full 90 minutes, and the five youngsters will step up to the U20 squad next season.

Another batch of young players will take their place in the U17s' squad next season, no doubt aiming to emulate the achievements of their predecessors over the past 12 months.

CELTIC YOUTH ACADEMY

CELTIC'S Academy has had a very rewarding season thanks to all the hard work from everyone involved in Coaching, Scouting, Sports Science, Medical, Administration, Education and Welfare.

The Academy operates to provide players for Celtic. The season past has proved to be very successful with five Academy players making their first-team debuts - Marcus Fraser, Paul George, Dylan McGeouch, Filip Twardzik and Tony Watt.

Playing with the championship-winning squad was a great boost for our players' development and will benefit them for the rest of their careers.

In addition we have now over 30 international players from Under-15s through to Under-19s..

Our Academy teams are split into three ages: The 17s-19s Professional Academy (Tommy McIntyre); the 13s to 16s Intermediate Academy (Michael O'Halloran); the 7s-12s Junior Academy (Martin Miller).

The U19s under the guidance of Tommy McIntyre and John Kennedy managed to win the Under-19 league and Youth Cup double for the third consecutive year. In addition we were unfortunate not to progress in our first outing at European football in the NextGen series, Celtic's group was Barcelona, Marseille and Manchester City where we finished with nine points and three wins.

The U15s, managed by Michael O'Halloran won the Nike Premier Cup, the equivalent of a British Cup, beating the likes of West Ham, Newcastle, Liverpool and Chelsea. They then progressed to the Nike Premier World Club Championship in Shanghai, China to play against the best teams from around the globe.

The Junior Academy manager is Martin Miller who oversees players as young as six and this is our starting point on the pathway of young Celtic players learning good habits on their journey and trying to fulfil their dreams of playing for Celtic.

Our Head Sports Scientist Ian Coll has put together an excellent training programme. The benefits have seen improvements throughout the Academy in speed, endurance, strength, core stability and injury prevention.

This helped our physiotherapists led by Rob Lee to work very closely with Ian and develop a strong partnership between medical and sports science in which the Academy

benefits from their combined expertise.

The partnership between Celtic and St Ninian's has now completed its third year. This partnership has gone from strength to strength with our players combining football and education. Season 2012/13 will see over 40 Academy players attend St Ninian's. When we started this programme we had 14 players but now we can see real benefits to our players with the same ethos and philosophy that education is at the core of the partnership.

Paul McLaughlin the Head at St Ninian's and his staff have been absolutely fantastic to work with and have made this programme a huge success. Brian Meehan, Welfare and Education officer, and Bill Reside, Liaison Officer, have worked very closely with the school and offering support to players and parents.

Lennoxtown Training Centre is utilised by the Academy to develop our young players.

It is important, however, not to forget our history and the Barrowfield training ground is an important part of that history where Celtic legends such as the Lisbon Lions, Henrik Larsson, Kenny Dalglish and Neil Lennon to name but a few, once graced this famous training pitch.

Our young players start at Barrowfield then progress to Lennoxtown and in the process learn that philosophy and ethos are of great importance in making them the player and person required to represent this great club and ultimately follow in the footsteps of such Celtic legends.

CHRIS McCART
Head of Youth and Academy

WOMEN'S FOOTBALL AT CELTIC

CELTIC'S very first women's team was established in June 2007 with an entry to the Scottish Women's Premier League.

Underpinning the women's first-team is a Development Squad which plays in the Scottish Women's Football League Division One as 'Celtic Reserves', and a Girls' Academy with teams at ages 17, 15, 13, 12 and 11 which compete in Scottish Women's Football regional girls' leagues.

In its four seasons in the Scottish Women's Premier League the first team has had three top-three finishes. In addition there has been a Scottish Cup final appearance and they have won the Premier League Cup.

In their first four seasons the Girls' Academy teams - at three age groups - won four Scottish Cups, 10 league cups and 11 league championships.

The Development Squad has an average age of 16. This is giving the very best players from the Girls' Academy an opportunity to gain experience at senior level. In previous seasons Celtic Reserves have won three championships out of four.

However, they could not be promoted as each club may have only one team in the Premier League. They have also won the Football League Cup.

In summer season 2011, the Celtic Girls' Academy recorded the following successes:

Celtic 17s: League Champions, Scottish Cup Winners
Celtic 15s: League Champions, Scottish Cup Winners, League Cup Winners
Celtic 13s: League Champions, League Cup Winners

For further information, or to ask for a trial for the senior women's teams or Girls' Academy teams, contact Paul Brownlie 0141 551 4430 or email pbrownlie@celticfc.co.uk.

If you wish to become involved and provide sponsorship for the female programme call Robert Docherty on 0141 551 4209 or email RobertDocherty@celticfc.co.uk.

FIRST-TEAM SQUAD

Goalkeepers
Gemma Fay
Chloe Logan

Defenders
Lauren MacMillan
Rebecca Bisland
Chloe Craig
Rhonda Jones
Michelle Barr
Fiona Brown

Midfielders and forwards
Megan Sneddon
Emily Thomson
Mairead Fulton
Natalie Ross
Heather Richards
Lisa Hendry
Jenna Ross
Hayley Cunningham
Suzanne Grant
Chloe Arthur

DEVELOPMENT SQUAD

COACHES: Danny McGrain, Steve Frail

BAHRUDIN ATAJIC

Atajic's family are from Bosnia but he was born in Sweden. He moved to Celtic from Malmo in January 2010 but suffered two long-term injuries shortly after. He's a versatile attacking player but he has found himself being used as a substitute more often than a regular starter.

JOE CHALMERS

Left-back, Chalmers, has been at Celtic since 10-years old and reached the first-team set-up during 2010/11. He started for the senior side in a friendly against Athletic Bilbao and was on the bench against Rennes last season. He has made good progress at 19s' and is a consistent player.

DARNEL FISHER

Celtic signed Darnel Fisher in 2011. The English teenager played for Reading-based Eldon Celtic before moving on to Farnborough. While he was on trial at the Hoops and went on to make the move permanent. He plays in central midfield, and also filled in at right-back last season.

JOHN HERRON

One of the most promising talents in the Youth Academy, Herron had an outstanding campaign last year. He provides a scoring threat for the team, taking his tally into double figures last season, and has good leadership qualities as well, having captained both the 16s and 17s to cup triumphs.

JACKSON IRVINE

The Australian joined the Hoops permanently in 2010 after a trial period. Wearing the captain's armband last season he lifted the league trophy and Scottish Youth Cup. Irvine plays in central midfield but has also featured in central defence where he can put in an equally reliable shift.

CALLUM McGREGOR

McGregor has been a crucial player for the 19s and was a big part of the treble double. He scored the goal which clinched the 2009/10 league, and netted a hat-trick in last season's Youth Cup final. He also made the bench in the Europa League away tie against Rennes.

PATRIK TWARDZIK

Like twin brother, Filip, he is blessed with tremendous ability and versatility. He was a regular goalscorer during his three Under-19 campaigns but he was unlucky to miss some of the big games last season, including early NextGen Series fixtures, and the Youth Cup final, due to niggling injuries.

CELTIC
STATISTICS

CELTIC TOP 10s

TOP 10 APPEARANCES

1	Billy McNeill	790
2	Paul McStay	677
3	Roy Aitken	672
4	Danny McGrain	663
5	Pat Bonner	641
6	Alec McNair	641
7	Bobby Lennox	586
8	Bobby Evans	537
9	Jimmy McMenemy	516
10	Jimmy Johnstone	515

Jimmy McMenemy

Alec McNair

TOP 10 LEAGUE APPEARANCES

1	Alec McNair	584
2	Paul McStay	514
3	Billy McNeill	486
4	Roy Aitken	483
5	Pat Bonner	483
6	Jimmy McMenemy	457
7	Danny McGrain	441
8	Patsy Gallacher	432
9	Charlie Shaw	420
10	Jimmy McStay	409

TOP 10 SCOTTISH CUP APPEARANCES

1	Billy McNeill	94
2	Jimmy McGrory	67
3	Paul McStay	66
4	Bobby Evans	64
5	Jimmy McStay	63
6	Danny McGrain	60
7	Jimmy McMenemy	59
8	Alec Thomson	59
9	Jimmy Quinn	58
10	Alec McNair	57

TOP 10 LEAGUE CUP APPEARANCES

1	Billy McNeill	138
2	Bobby Lennox	120
3	Danny McGrain	106
4	Jimmy Johnstone	92
5	Bobby Evans	88
6	Roy Aitken	84
7	Bobby Murdoch	84
8	Bertie Peacock	80
9	Tommy Gemmell	74
10	Tommy Burns	70

TOP 10 EUROPEAN APPEARANCES

1	Billy McNeill	72
2	Bobby Lennox	69
3	Jimmy Johnstone	67
4	Henrik Larsson	58
5	Bobby Murdoch	57
6	Danny McGrain	56
7	Tommy Gemmell	54
8	Neil Lennon	53
9	Jackie McNamara	51
10	Stilian Petrov	51

Billy McNeill

Henrik Larsson and Neil Lennon

TOP 10 SCORERS

1	Jimmy McGrory	468
2	Bobby Lennox	273
3	Henrik Larsson	242
4	Stevie Chalmers	231
5	Jimmy Quinn	217
6	Patsy Gallacher	192
7	John Hughes	189
8	Sandy McMahon	177
9	Jimmy McMenemy	168
10	Kenny Dalglish	167

TOP 10 LEAGUE SCORERS

1	Jimmy McGrory	395
2	Jimmy Quinn	187
3	Patsy Gallacher	186
4	Henrik Larsson	174
5	Bobby Lennox	170
6	Stevie Chalmers	158
7	Jimmy McMenemy	141
8	Sandy McMahon	130
9	Adam McLean	128
10	Jimmy McColl	117

TOP 10 SCOTTISH CUP SCORERS

1	Jimmy McGrory	73
2	Sandy McMahon	47
3	Stevie Chalmers	33
4	Bobby Lennox	31
5	Jimmy Quinn	30
6	Johnny Campbell	25
7	John Hughes	25
8	Henrik Larsson	23
9	Jimmy McMenemy	23
10	Adam McLean	20

Jimmy McGrory

Jimmy Quinn

TOP 10 LEAGUE CUP SCORERS

1	Bobby Lennox	62
2	John Hughes	38
3	Kenny Dalglish	35
4	Stevie Chalmers	27
5	Bobby Collins	26
6	Charlie Nicholas	26
7	Joe McBride	24
8	Harry Hood	22
9	Billy McPhail	22
10	Jimmy Johnstone	21
	John McPhail	21
	Willie Wallace	21

Pat Bonner

TOP 10 EUROPEAN SCORERS

1 Henrik Larsson	35
2 Jimmy Johnstone	16
3 Chris Sutton	16
4 Bobby Lennox	14
5 Stevie Chlamers	13
6 Willie Wallace	13
7 Tommy Gemmell	12
8 Harry Hood	12
9 Bobby Murdoch	11
10 John Hughes	10

TOP 10 SUBSTITUTE APPEARANCES

1 Shaun Maloney	91
2 Bobby Lennox	79
3 Georgios Samaras	64
4 Aiden McGeady	54
5 Paddy McCourt	52
6 Jackie McNamara	52
7 Simon Donnelly	50
8 Andy Walker	50
9 Paul Wilson	49
10 Brian McLaughlin	48

TOP 10 GOALKEEPING APPEARANCES

1 Pat Bonner	641
2 Charlie Shaw	436
3 Joe Kennaway	295
4 Davie Adams	291
5 Peter Latchford	275
6 Artur Boruc	221
7 Frank Haffey	201
8 John Fallon	195
9 Ronnie Simpson	188
10 John Thomson	188

Chris Sutton

	LEAGUE			LG CUP			SCOT CUP			EUROPE			TOTAL		
	A	S	G	A	S	G	A	S	G	A	S	G	A	S	G
McNeill, Billy	486	0	21	138	0	4	94	0	7	72	0	3	790	0	35
McStay, Paul	509	6	57	54	0	7	66	0	6	42	0	2	671	6	72
Aitken, Roy	483	0	40	82	2	6	55	0	2	50	0	4	670	2	52
McGrain, Danny	433	8	4	105	1	3	60	0	1	55	1	0	653	10	8
Bonner, Pat	483	0	0	64	0	0	55	0	0	39	0	0	641	0	0
McNair, Alec	584	0	9	0	0	0	57	0	0	0	0	0	641	0	9
Lennox, Bobby	297	49	170	107	13	62	46	5	31	57	12	14	507	79	277
Evans, Bobby	385	0	10	88	0	1	64	0	0	0	0	0	537	0	11
McMenemy, Jimmy	457	0	141	0	0	0	59	0	23	0	0	0	516	0	164
Johnstone, Jimmy	298	10	82	87	5	21	47	1	11	66	1	16	498	17	130
Burns, Tommy	324	32	52	70	0	15	38	5	12	31	3	3	463	40	82
Murdoch, Bobby	287	4	61	84	0	17	53	0	13	57	0	11	481	4	102
Grant, Peter	338	26	15	40	3	3	34	4	1	32	1	0	444	34	19
McStay, Jimmy	409	0	6	0	0	0	63	0	2	0	0	0	472	0	8
Gallacher, Patsy	432	0	186	0	0	0	32	0	6	0	0	0	464	0	192
Peacock, Bertie	319	0	32	80	0	10	56	0	8	0	0	0	455	0	50
Thomson, Alec	392	0	87	0	0	0	59	0	13	0	0	0	451	0	100
McStay, Willie 1912	399	0	37	0	0	0	47	0	2	0	0	0	446	0	39
McGrory, Jimmy	378	0	395	0	0	0	67	0	73	0	0	0	445	0	468
Young, Jim 1903	392	0	14	0	0	0	51	0	0	0	0	0	443	0	14
McAtee, Andy	407	0	65	0	0	0	32	0	2	0	0	0	439	0	67
Shaw, Charlie	420	0	0	0	0	0	16	0	0	0	0	0	436	0	0
Gemmell, Tommy	247	0	38	74	0	10	43	0	3	54	0	12	418	0	63
McLean, Adam	367	0	128	0	0	0	41	0	20	0	0	0	408	0	148
Boyd, Tom	296	10	2	31	2	0	31	3	0	33	1	0	391	16	2
Chalmers, Steve	253	8	158	57	2	27	45	2	33	38	1	13	393	13	231
Wilson, Peter	344	0	14	0	0	0	51	0	1	0	0	0	395	0	15
MacLeod, Murdo	274	7	55	44	0	13	36	2	7	32	0	7	386	9	82
Hughes, John 1959	233	3	115	62	1	38	42	1	25	40	1	10	377	6	188

	LEAGUE			LG CUP			SCOT CUP			EUROPE			TOTAL		
	A	S	G	A	S	G	A	S	G	A	S	G	A	S	G
Dodds, Joe	351	0	28	0	0	0	27	0	2	0	0	0	378	0	30
McAdam, Tom	251	7	36	45	1	7	30	2	3	28	1	0	354	11	46
McNamara, Jackie '95	221	36	10	17	2	1	26	5	3	43	9	1	307	52	15
Brogan, Jim	208	5	6	55	2	2	37	1	0	32	1	1	332	9	9
Quinn, Jimmy 1901	273	0	187	0	0	0	58	0	30	0	0	0	331	0	217
McGonagle, Peter	286	0	8	0	0	0	39	0	1	0	0	0	325	0	9
Hogg, Bobby	278	0	0	10	0	0	34	0	0	0	0	0	322	0	0
Collins, Bobby	220	0	81	62	0	26	38	0	10	0	0	0	320	0	117
Dalglish, Kenny	200	4	112	56	3	35	30	0	11	27	0	9	313	7	167
Geatons, Charlie	286	0	11	0	0	0	33	0	0	0	0	0	319	0	11
Tully, Charlie	216	0	30	68	0	7	35	0	6	0	0	0	319	0	43
Fernie, Willie	219	0	54	59	0	11	39	0	10	0	0	0	317	0	75
Clark, John 1958	185	1	1	60	2	1	30	1	1	37	0	0	312	4	3
Larsson, Henrik	218	3	174	11	0	10	25	0	23	58	0	35	312	3	242
Hood, Harry	161	28	74	53	9	22	25	4	13	24	6	12	263	47	121
Loney, Willie	254	0	28	0	0	0	51	0	2	0	0	0	305	0	30
McFarlane, John	268	0	12	0	0	0	36	0	2	0	0	0	304	0	14
Lennon, Neil	212	2	3	10	1	0	26	0	0	52	1	0	300	4	3
Provan, Davie	192	14	28	41	1	10	29	0	2	25	1	2	287	16	42
Connolly, Paddy	259	0	40	0	0	0	37	0	7	0	0	0	296	0	47
Kennaway, Joe	263	0	0	0	0	0	32	0	0	0	0	0	295	0	0
Adams, Davie	248	0	0	0	0	0	43	0	0	0	0	0	291	0	0
Latchford, Peter	186	0	0	39	0	0	27	0	0	23	0	0	275	0	0
Whyte, Derek	211	5	7	18	0	0	26	0	0	15	0	1	270	5	8
Auld, Bertie	167	9	50	42	5	20	26	2	8	22	2	0	257	18	78
Collins, John	211	6	47	22	0	3	21	0	3	13	0	1	267	6	54
Lambert, Paul	180	12	14	10	1	2	19	4	1	44	3	2	253	20	19
Mochan, Neil	191	0	81	43	0	12	34	0	16	0	0	0	268	0	109
Petrov, Stiliyan	172	13	55	9	5	0	15	3	5	49	2	4	245	23	64

	LEAGUE			LG CUP			SCOT CUP			EUROPE			TOTAL		
	A	S	G	A	S	G	A	S	G	A	S	G	A	S	G
Callaghan, Tommy	143	14	14	47	6	8	24	2	6	26	2	6	240	24	34
Hamilton, Davie	221	0	53	0	0	0	39	0	7	0	0	0	260	0	60
Hay, James	214	0	14	0	0	0	41	0	5	0	0	0	255	0	19
MacDonald, Roddy	160	5	21	48	2	4	21	0	3	19	0	5	248	7	33
Fallon, Sean	177	0	8	46	0	3	31	0	2	0	0	0	254	0	13
Connelly, George	129	7	5	60	3	4	24	1	2	28	2	2	241	13	13
McGeady, Aiden	147	38	31	9	4	3	15	6	1	27	6	2	198	54	37
Nicholas, Charlie	159	28	85	24	7	26	9	2	7	17	3	7	209	40	125
McGarvey, Frank	159	9	77	29	6	11	20	4	13	18	0	8	226	19	109
Kennedy, Jim	170	0	0	31	0	2	29	0	0	11	0	0	241	0	2
MacKay, Duncan	162	0	0	37	0	0	33	0	0	4	0	0	236	0	0
Balde, Bobo	160	1	9	14	0	5	14	0	2	45	0	1	233	1	17
Haughney, Mike	159	0	32	45	0	7	29	0	5	0	0	0	233	0	44
Johnstone, Peter	211	0	23	0	0	0	22	0	2	0	0	0	233	0	25
Divers, John 1956	171	0	78	26	0	8	28	0	11	7	0	3	232	0	100
Wallace, Willie	135	6	88	31	5	21	24	2	12	27	2	13	217	15	134
Craig, Jim	143	4	1	29	1	4	21	2	0	31	0	1	224	7	6
Thompson, Alan	146	12	37	8	3	2	19	1	4	34	4	8	207	20	51
Boruc, Artur	162	0	0	12	0	0	15	0	0	32	0	0	221	0	0
Somers, Peter	186	0	52	0	0	0	33	0	10	0	0	0	219	0	62
McMaster, John	204	0	6	0	0	0	14	0	0	0	0	0	218	0	6
Browning, John	210	0	64	0	0	0	7	0	2	0	0	0	217	0	66
McMahon, Sandy	174	0	130	0	0	0	43	0	47	0	0	0	217	0	177
Wilson, Paul	97	36	30	40	8	15	14	1	4	17	4	6	168	49	55
Campbell, John	169	0	88	0	0	0	46	0	25	0	0	0	215	0	113
Maloney, Shaun	89	69	39	11	4	8	5	5	2	19	13	3	124	91	52
Cringan, Willie	202	0	9	0	0	0	12	0	0	0	0	0	214	0	9
McInally, Tommy	188	0	110	0	0	0	25	0	16	0	0	0	213	0	126
Orr, Willie	165	0	17	0	0	0	47	0	6	0	0	0	212	0	23

	LEAGUE			LG CUP			SCOT CUP			EUROPE			TOTAL		
	A	S	G	A	S	G	A	S	G	A	S	G	A	S	G
Crum, Johnny	190	0	73	0	0	0	21	0	14	0	0	0	211	0	87
Morris, Chris	156	6	8	16	1	0	22	0	1	9	0	0	203	7	9
McCluskey, George	110	32	55	25	7	11	13	4	12	13	3	5	161	46	83
Cassidy, Joe 1912	189	0	90	0	0	0	15	0	13	0	0	0	204	0	103
McPhail, John	142	0	58	38	0	21	24	0	13	0	0	0	204	0	92
McManus, Stephen	148	2	18	12	0	1	11	0	0	29	1	2	200	3	21
Haffey, Frank	140	0	0	24	0	0	34	0	0	3	0	0	201	0	0
Hartson, John	125	21	89	10	1	7	11	1	8	25	7	6	171	30	110
Napier, Charlie	176	0	82	0	0	0	24	0	10	0	0	0	200	0	92
Mjallby, Johan	133	12	13	10	0	1	14	2	0	28	0	1	185	14	15
McClair, Brian	129	16	99	19	1	9	14	4	11	13	3	2	175	24	121
Sutton, Chris	127	3	60	8	1	2	16	0	5	41	2	16	192	6	83
Brown, Scott	132	9	14	9	1	2	16	1	4	27	2	0	184	13	20
Donnelly, Simon	113	33	31	11	6	4	9	4	2	13	7	6	146	50	43
Fallon, John	125	0	0	36	0	0	14	0	0	20	0	0	195	0	0

Scott Brown, who has the most Celtic appearances of the current squad, in his trademark celebration pose

	LEAGUE			LG CUP			SCOT CUP			EUROPE			TOTAL		
	A	S	G	A	S	G	A	S	G	A	S	G	A	S	G
Hilley, Hugh	171	0	0	0	0	0	24	0	0	0	0	0	195	0	0
Paterson, George	175	0	9	0	0	0	20	0	1	0	0	0	195	0	10
Edvaldsson, Shuggie	120	9	26	35	2	8	12	1	0	16	0	4	183	12	38
Walker, Andy	112	38	49	15	7	10	11	2	6	7	3	4	145	50	69
Hay, Davie	106	3	6	37	0	5	24	0	1	23	0	0	190	3	12
Lynch, Andy	124	7	15	31	1	6	13	0	4	16	0	0	184	8	25
Miller, Joe	113	31	27	8	5	2	24	2	3	5	4	1	150	42	33
McCluskey, Pat	105	11	10	35	6	1	12	2	1	17	3	1	169	22	13
Simpson, Ronnie	118	0	0	29	0	0	17	0	0	24	0	0	188	0	0
Thomson, John	163	0	0	0	0	0	25	0	0	0	0	0	188	0	0
Deans, Dixie	122	5	89	21	1	11	21	0	18	11	3	6	175	9	124
Bonnar, John	120	0	0	38	0	0	22	0	0	0	0	0	180	0	0
Agathe, Didier	109	11	9	4	0	0	16	0	0	39	1	2	168	12	11
Samaras, Georgios	80	46	37	4	4	5	11	8	3	21	6	4	116	64	49
Morrison, John	161	0	1	0	0	0	17	0	0	0	0	0	178	0	1
Reid, Mark	120	4	5	21	2	6	17	0	1	12	1	0	170	7	12
Valgaeren, Joos	112	2	7	9	0	0	12	1	1	36	4	2	169	7	10
Galloway, Mike	113	23	8	17	2	0	7	3	0	9	0	2	146	28	10
Gallagher, Charlie	107	0	17	28	0	11	23	0	4	13	0	0	171	0	32
McColl, Jimmy	165	0	117	0	0	0	4	0	6	0	0	0	169	0	123
Nakamura, Shunsuke	121	7	29	7	0	1	12	0	1	17	2	2	157	9	33
Lyon, Willie	146	0	16	0	0	0	17	0	1	0	0	0	163	0	17
Douglas, Rab	107	1	0	7	0	0	17	0	0	30	0	0	161	1	0
Murphy, Frank	144	0	46	0	0	0	17	0	4	0	0	0	161	0	50
Rogan, Anton	115	12	4	12	1	0	15	0	0	6	0	1	148	13	5
Delaney, Jimmy	143	0	69	0	0	0	17	0	5	0	0	0	160	0	74
Boden, Alec	122	0	2	20	0	0	16	0	0	0	0	0	158	0	2
Gould, Jonathan	109	1	0	12	1	0	11	0	0	24	0	0	156	2	0
Beattie, Dick	114	0	0	28	0	0	14	0	0	0	0	0	156	0	0

	LEAGUE			LG CUP			SCOT CUP			EUROPE			TOTAL		
	A	S	G	A	S	G	A	S	G	A	S	G	A	S	G
McLeod, Donald	131	0	0	0	0	0	24	0	0	0	0	0	155	0	0
Glavin, Ronnie	100	2	36	26	4	4	11	1	8	10	1	2	147	8	50
O'Neil, Brian	92	28	8	6	4	1	12	1	0	9	3	1	119	36	10
Bennett, Alec	126	0	44	0	0	0	26	0	6	0	0	0	152	0	50
McNally, Mark	112	10	3	11	2	1	10	0	0	6	1	0	139	13	4
Baillie, Joe	107	0	0	31	0	1	13	0	0	0	0	0	151	0	1
Caldwell, Gary	105	1	5	8	0	0	7	1	2	28	1	0	148	3	7
Stein, Jock	106	0	2	21	0	0	21	0	0	0	0	0	148	0	2
Williams, Evan	82	0	0	25	0	0	19	0	0	22	0	0	148	0	0
MacDonald, Malcolm	134	0	31	0	0	0	13	0	5	0	0	0	147	0	36
Wdowczyk, Dariusz	112	4	4	11	0	0	13	0	2	6	1	0	142	5	6
Walsh, Jimmy	108	0	45	21	0	8	15	0	5	0	0	0	144	0	58
Stubbs, Alan	101	4	4	8	1	0	11	0	0	18	1	2	138	6	6
Doyle, Johnny	82	13	15	25	4	14	10	2	7	6	1	1	123	20	37
Naylor, Lee	95	5	3	5	0	0	12	0	0	22	3	0	134	8	3
Creaney, Gerry	85	28	36	9	1	7	9	1	8	6	3	2	109	33	53
McKinlay, Tosh	87	13	0	4	2	0	17	2	0	15	1	0	123	18	0
Kelly, James	104	0	3	0	0	0	35	0	1	0	0	0	139	0	4
Battles, Barney	110	0	6	0	0	0	26	0	0	0	0	0	136	0	6
Marshall, Gordon '92	101	0	0	14	0	0	9	0	0	12	0	0	136	0	0
Buchan, Willie	120	0	38	0	0	0	14	0	7	0	0	0	134	0	45
Gilchrist, John	127	0	7	0	0	0	7	0	0	0	0	0	134	0	7
Doyle, Dan	112	0	3	0	0	0	21	0	2	0	0	0	133	0	5
Milne, Roy	108	0	0	20	0	0	5	0	0	0	0	0	133	0	0
Young, Ian	84	0	2	21	0	1	13	0	0	15	0	0	133	0	3
Wilson, Mark	87	11	2	7	1	0	7	1	1	17	2	0	118	15	3
Thomson, Bertie	113	0	22	0	0	0	18	0	8	0	0	0	131	0	30
Coyne, Tommy	82	23	43	5	1	1	13	2	8	4	1	0	104	27	52
Smith, Eric	95	0	13	16	0	3	19	0	4	0	0	0	130	0	20

	LEAGUE			LG CUP			SCOT CUP			EUROPE			TOTAL		
	A	S	G	A	S	G	A	S	G	A	S	G	A	S	G
McDonald, Scott	84	4	51	7	1	4	7	0	4	20	6	6	118	11	65
Moravcik, Lubo	75	19	29	8	2	2	9	1	1	11	4	3	103	26	35
Johnston, Maurice	97	2	52	8	0	9	14	0	6	6	0	4	125	2	71
Miller, Willie	94	0	0	23	0	0	6	0	0	0	0	0	123	0	0
O'Donnell, Phil	76	14	16	6	1	0	12	4	4	7	1	1	101	20	21
Crerand, Pat	91	0	5	13	0	1	14	0	1	2	0	1	120	0	8
McArthur, Dan	104	0	0	0	0	0	16	0	0	0	0	0	120	0	0
Sullivan, Dom	83	7	10	12	1	1	8	1	0	6	1	1	109	10	12
Madden, Johnny	92	0	33	0	0	0	26	0	16	0	0	0	118	0	49
Mallan, Jimmy	90	0	0	21	0	0	6	0	0	0	0	0	117	0	0
Meechan, Frank	86	0	0	11	0	0	19	0	0	0	0	0	116	0	0
Varga, Stanislav	79	1	10	3	1	1	10	0	2	21	0	1	113	2	14
McGhee, Mark	62	26	27	4	1	1	10	6	4	4	2	2	80	35	34
Wieghorst, Morten	59	24	10	7	3	2	5	4	2	8	3	2	79	34	16
Scarff, Peter	97	0	51	0	0	0	15	0	4	0	0	0	112	0	55
Cook, Willie	100	0	0	0	0	0	10	0	0	0	0	0	110	0	0
Mahe, Stephane	74	3	4	10	0	0	9	0	1	14	0	0	107	3	5
McAulay, Pat	78	0	4	22	0	0	9	0	0	0	0	0	109	0	4
Ven of Hess, Jan	63	15	34	4	1	1	11	0	7	11	3	2	89	19	44
Weir, Jock	81	0	26	10	0	2	15	0	9	0	0	0	106	0	37
McAvennie, Frank	82	3	37	7	0	8	10	0	4	4	0	1	103	3	50
Shevlin, Peter	86	0	0	0	0	0	17	0	0	0	0	0	103	0	0
Hinkel, Andreas	78	1	1	5	0	0	8	0	0	11	0	0	102	1	1
Mowbray, Tony	78	3	5	7	0	0	9	0	0	6	0	0	100	3	5
Macari, Lou	50	8	27	19	5	14	8	0	8	12	0	8	89	13	57
Murray, Steve	62	1	11	20	0	5	8	0	4	10	0	1	100	1	21
Thom, Andreas	57	13	14	9	2	4	6	2	2	12	0	7	84	17	27
Byrne, Alec	70	0	22	9	0	0	19	0	8	2	0	0	100	0	30
Sneddon, Alan	66	0	1	15	0	0	9	0	0	10	0	0	100	0	1

	LEAGUE			LG CUP			SCOT CUP			EUROPE			TOTAL		
	A	S	G	A	S	G	A	S	G	A	S	G	A	S	G
Blessington, Jimmy	82	0	31	0	0	0	17	0	8	0	0	0	99	0	39
Reynolds, Jerry	74	0	0	0	0	0	25	0	0	0	0	0	99	0	0
Brown, Hugh	98	0	2	0	0	0	0	0	0	0	0	0	98	0	2
McLaughlin, Brian '92	38	37	5	1	4	0	9	4	0	2	3	0	50	48	5
Maley, Willie	75	0	0	0	0	0	21	0	1	0	0	0	96	0	1
Weir, James	82	0	1	0	0	0	14	0	0	0	0	0	96	0	1
Mitchell, John	89	0	0	0	0	0	6	0	0	0	0	0	95	0	0
Fulton, Steve	54	22	2	7	2	1	4	2	0	2	2	0	67	28	3
Burley, Craig	61	3	20	7	0	2	6	0	1	16	0	2	90	3	25
McBride, Joe	52	3	54	21	0	24	8	0	3	9	0	5	90	3	86
Kivlichan, Willie	76	0	20	0	0	0	16	0	7	0	0	0	92	0	27
van Hooijdonk, Pierre	66	2	44	5	1	3	11	0	9	5	2	0	87	5	56
Conroy, Mike 1978	59	9	7	8	5	1	5	1	1	4	1	0	76	16	9
Forster, Fraser	69	0	0	8	0	0	7	0	0	7	0	0	91	0	0
Hunter, Alistair	60	0	0	17	0	0	10	0	0	4	0	0	91	0	0
O'Donnell, Hugh	75	0	20	0	0	0	15	0	7	0	0	0	90	0	27
Loovens, Glenn	57	4	8	5	1	1	6	0	0	17	0	0	85	5	9
McStay, Willie 1979	55	12	2	11	1	0	7	0	0	4	0	0	77	13	2
McInally, Alan	38	28	17	6	6	5	4	1	1	3	2	0	51	37	23
Divers, Johnny 1893	64	0	37	0	0	0	23	0	8	0	0	0	87	0	45
Ledley, Joe	57	4	9	8	0	1	8	0	4	10	0	1	83	4	15
Ki Sung Yueng	44	22	9	3	3	0	6	0	1	8	1	1	61	26	11
Archdeacon, Owen	38	38	7	1	4	1	3	1	0	0	2	0	42	45	8
Hartley, Paul	53	9	3	3	1	0	6	1	0	12	1	1	74	12	4
Hooper, Gary	60	2	44	8	0	3	8	0	1	5	2	3	81	4	51
Higgins, John	65	0	31	7	0	3	12	0	7	0	0	0	84	0	41
Russell, Davie	71	0	12	0	0	0	13	0	0	0	0	0	84	0	12
Gillespie, Gary	67	2	3	3	0	0	4	0	0	8	0	0	82	2	3
O'Donnell, Frank	78	0	51	0	0	0	5	0	7	0	0	0	83	0	58

	LEAGUE			LG CUP			SCOT CUP			EUROPE			TOTAL		
	A	S	G	A	S	G	A	S	G	A	S	G	A	S	G
Stark, Billy	58	6	17	3	1	4	7	3	3	5	0	1	73	10	25
Divers, John 1932	75	0	44	0	0	0	7	0	4	0	0	0	82	0	48
O'Neill, Willie	49	1	0	18	2	0	3	0	0	9	0	0	79	3	0
Stokes, Anthony	47	16	26	7	0	8	3	4	4	4	1	2	61	21	40
Petta, Bobby	36	16	0	3	4	1	3	1	1	14	4	1	56	25	3
Mulgrew, Charlie	49	4	8	5	2	1	10	0	2	8	1	1	72	7	12
Carroll, Bobby	61	0	21	12	0	4	4	0	1	1	0	1	78	0	27
Sylla, Momo	26	20	3	3	3	1	3	2	2	5	14	1	37	39	7
Pearson, Stephen	22	34	6	3	1	0	5	1	0	6	4	1	36	40	7
Sinclair, Graeme	45	6	1	10	2	0	3	2	0	7	0	0	65	10	1
Jackson, Mike	57	0	23	8	0	4	8	0	3	1	0	0	74	0	30
Price, Billy	51	0	0	13	0	0	10	0	0	0	0	0	74	0	0
Cullen, Joe	58	0	0	0	0	0	15	0	0	0	0	0	73	0	0
Telfer, Paul	56	1	1	5	0	0	3	0	0	7	1	0	71	2	1
Riseth, Vidar	54	2	3	5	0	1	4	0	0	7	1	1	70	3	5
Craig, Joe	53	1	24	5	2	4	7	1	7	4	0	0	69	4	35
Zurawski, Maciej	42	14	22	4	1	5	1	1	3	6	4	0	53	20	30
Paton, Johnny	52	0	11	15	0	3	5	0	2	0	0	0	72	0	16
Wilson, Sammy	48	0	26	14	0	13	8	0	7	0	0	0	70	0	46
O'Dea, Darren	35	14	4	3	0	1	8	2	1	3	5	0	49	21	6
Blinker, Regi	37	11	9	6	0	2	6	1	1	8	0	0	57	12	12
Forrest, James	38	12	11	4	0	2	2	3	0	7	3	0	51	18	13
Jack, John	48	0	0	12	0	0	8	0	0	0	0	0	68	0	0
McCourt, Paddy	11	39	9	1	4	1	2	5	0	2	4	0	16	52	10
Elliott, Paul	52	0	2	5	0	3	8	0	0	1	0	0	66	0	5
Majstorovic, Daniel	47	2	1	4	0	0	4	1	1	8	0	0	63	3	2
Dziekanowski, Jacki	42	6	10	9	0	7	7	0	1	2	0	4	60	6	22
Davidson, Vic	37	2	17	9	1	2	2	3	2	6	6	3	54	12	24
Beattie, Craig	18	32	13	3	2	2	0	4	0	1	5	1	22	43	16

	LEAGUE			LG CUP			SCOT CUP			EUROPE			TOTAL		
	A	S	G	A	S	G	A	S	G	A	S	G	A	S	G
McCarthy, Mick	48	0	0	3	0	0	8	0	1	5	0	0	64	0	1
Lynch, Matt	48	0	3	6	0	0	9	0	0	0	0	0	63	0	3
Smith, Jamie	12	31	2	6	1	2	3	1	1	2	7	0	23	40	5
King, Alex	56	0	11	0	0	0	6	0	2	0	0	0	62	0	13
Burchill, Mark	15	34	20	3	2	0	1	2	1	4	1	3	23	39	24
Hannah, David	28	14	0	2	1	0	3	4	0	7	2	1	40	21	1
Corbett, Willie	48	0	0	7	0	0	5	0	0	0	0	0	60	0	0
Dunbar, Tom	51	0	3	0	0	0	9	0	1	0	0	0	60	0	4
Brattbakk, Harald	27	17	12	0	0	0	5	2	4	7	2	4	39	21	20
Rollo, Alec	37	0	1	13	0	0	9	0	1	0	0	0	59	0	2
McGinlay, Pat	44	3	11	5	2	2	1	0	0	4	0	0	54	5	13
McGugan, Paul	45	4	2	5	0	0	1	1	0	3	0	0	54	5	2
Colrain, John	44	0	21	4	0	2	10	0	0	0	0	0	58	0	23
McGrory, John	38	0	3	9	0	0	11	0	8	0	0	0	58	0	11
Watson, Hugh	49	0	0	0	0	0	9	0	1	0	0	0	58	0	1
Kayal, Beram	36	4	2	4	0	0	5	0	0	9	0	0	54	4	2
McPhail, Billy	33	0	14	20	0	22	4	0	4	0	0	0	57	0	40
Laursen, Ulrik	33	6	0	4	0	0	5	0	0	7	2	0	49	8	0
Robson, Barry	33	11	4	1	1	0	0	1	0	8	2	3	42	15	7
Connaghan, Denis	32	0	0	15	0	0	4	0	0	5	0	0	56	0	0
Davidson, Robert	43	0	0	0	0	0	13	0	0	0	0	0	56	0	0
Izaguirre, Emilio	42	3	1	5	0	0	6	0	0	0	0	0	53	3	1
Conn, Alfie	34	3	10	8	1	3	6	0	0	3	1	0	51	5	13
Slater, Stuart	40	4	3	3	0	0	3	0	0	4	0	0	50	6	3
Vata, Rudi	33	12	4	3	0	0	4	0	0	4	0	0	44	12	4
Crainey, Stephen	19	20	0	6	1	1	2	3	0	3	2	0	30	26	1
Donati, Massimo	25	5	3	4	0	0	3	2	0	11	4	2	43	11	5
Commons, Kris	27	11	12	2	2	1	7	1	2	1	3	0	37	17	15
MacKay, Malcolm	32	5	4	5	1	0	4	0	2	4	1	0	45	7	6

	LEAGUE			LG CUP			SCOT CUP			EUROPE			TOTAL		
	A	S	G	A	S	G	A	S	G	A	S	G	A	S	G
Crosas, Mark	28	8	1	3	1	0	7	1	0	4	0	0	42	10	1
Tebily, Olivier	29	9	0	4	1	1	2	1	0	6	0	1	41	11	2
Johnson, Tommy	23	12	18	3	1	3	2	5	1	2	4	3	30	22	25
Mulrooney, John	42	0	0	0	0	0	9	0	0	0	0	0	51	0	0
O'Leary, Pierce	38	2	1	1	2	0	5	1	0	0	2	0	44	7	1
Donoghue, John	42	0	1	0	0	0	8	0	0	0	0	0	50	0	1
Gilhooly, Pat	46	0	17	0	0	0	4	0	3	0	0	0	50	0	20
Marshall, David	34	1	0	2	0	0	3	1	0	8	1	0	47	3	0
Wallace, Ross	18	17	1	3	1	3	2	2	0	1	6	0	24	26	4
Dowds, Peter	36	0	16	0	0	0	13	0	3	0	0	0	49	0	19
Cadete, Jorge	32	5	30	3	0	5	5	0	2	4	0	1	44	5	38
Falconer, Willie	33	8	5	1	1	0	4	2	3	0	0	0	38	11	8
Annoni, Enrico	26	11	0	0	3	0	6	1	0	1	1	0	33	16	0
Guppy, Steve	22	11	0	3	0	0	4	0	0	4	5	0	33	16	0
Sno, Evander	10	20	1	2	2	0	3	2	0	5	5	0	20	29	1
Brogan, Frank	37	0	0	1	0	0	9	0	0	1	0	0	48	0	0
Rieper, Marc	37	0	2	2	0	1	4	0	0	5	0	0	48	0	3
Viduka, Mark	36	1	30	4	0	1	3	0	3	4	0	1	47	1	35
McNamara, Jackie '72	19	3	2	16	4	2	2	0	1	3	1	0	40	8	5
Bogan, Tommy	34	0	5	9	0	3	4	0	0	0	0	0	47	0	8
Livingstone, Dugald	44	0	0	0	0	0	3	0	0	0	0	0	47	0	0
Wilson, James	47	0	0	0	0	0	0	0	0	0	0	0	47	0	0
Hughes, John 1995	31	1	2	5	0	0	3	0	0	7	0	0	46	1	2
Jarosik, Jiri	24	9	5	1	0	0	2	0	0	8	3	2	35	12	7
Melrose, Jim	20	9	7	6	2	3	2	2	1	3	3	0	31	16	11
Healy, Colin	16	13	1	5	1	2	3	1	0	3	5	0	27	20	3
Bell, John	35	0	16	0	0	0	11	0	7	0	0	0	46	0	23
Marshall, Harry	29	0	5	0	0	0	17	0	0	0	0	0	46	0	5
Rogne, Thomas	32	5	2	5	0	1	4	0	0	0	0	0	41	5	3

	LEAGUE			LG CUP			SCOT CUP			EUROPE			TOTAL		
	A	S	G	A	S	G	A	S	G	A	S	G	A	S	G
Miller, Kenny	21	12	7	0	1	0	2	2	1	5	3	3	28	18	11
Payton, Andy	20	16	15	3	2	5	1	1	0	3	0	0	27	19	20
Jackson, Darren	13	16	3	3	0	1	0	3	1	6	5	2	22	24	7
Gallagher, Paddy	30	0	0	0	0	0	15	0	1	0	0	0	45	0	1
Fortune, Marc-Antoine	24	8	10	0	0	0	2	1	0	6	4	2	32	13	12
Kennedy, John 1999	19	9	1	4	1	0	1	1	0	7	3	0	31	14	1
McVittie, Matt	33	0	11	6	0	0	5	0	3	0	0	0	44	0	14
Stanton, Pat	37	0	0	0	0	0	7	0	0	0	0	0	44	0	0
Welford, Jim	38	0	0	0	0	0	6	0	0	0	0	0	44	0	0
Fillipi, Joe	30	2	0	8	0	0	2	1	0	1	0	0	41	3	0
Cha, Du-Ri	25	6	2	2	1	0	1	0	0	9	0	0	37	7	2
Conway, Jim	32	0	9	10	0	4	1	0	0	0	0	0	43	0	13
Donnelly, John	31	0	0	9	0	0	3	0	0	0	0	0	43	0	0
Nguemo, Landry	30	0	0	1	0	0	3	0	0	9	0	0	43	0	0
Miller, Liam	13	12	2	1	1	0	0	1	0	5	10	3	19	24	5
Carruth, Joe	39	0	27	0	0	0	3	0	2	0	0	0	42	0	29
Hodge, John	34	0	19	0	0	0	8	0	5	0	0	0	42	0	24
Kerr, Stuart	34	1	0	0	0	0	6	0	0	0	1	0	40	2	0
Berkovic, Eyal	29	3	9	0	2	0	1	0	0	4	3	3	34	8	12
Wanyama, Victor	24	5	4	2	2	0	2	2	0	5	0	0	33	9	4
Cushley, John	30	0	0	5	0	0	1	0	0	5	0	0	41	0	0
Quinn, Jimmy 1964	23	5	1	9	0	0	2	1	0	1	0	0	35	6	1
McCallum, Denis	39	0	3	0	0	0	1	0	0	0	0	0	40	0	3
Storrier, Dave	34	0	0	0	0	0	6	0	0	0	0	0	40	0	0
Killen, Chris	4	22	2	2	1	1	0	1	0	2	8	0	8	32	3
Gallagher, Willie	29	0	0	6	0	3	4	0	0	0	0	0	39	0	3
Hunter, George	31	0	0	0	0	0	7	0	0	0	0	0	38	0	0
McNamee, John	27	0	0	2	0	0	7	0	0	2	0	0	38	0	0
Moir, James	34	0	0	0	0	0	4	0	0	0	0	0	38	0	0

	LEAGUE			LG CUP			SCOT CUP			EUROPE			TOTAL		
	A	S	G	A	S	G	A	S	G	A	S	G	A	S	G
Murphy, James B	35	0	0	0	0	0	3	0	0	0	0	0	38	0	0
Shepherd, Tony	16	12	3	2	3	0	1	1	0	3	0	0	22	16	3
Hedman, Magnus	26	0	0	1	0	0	1	0	0	9	0	0	37	0	0
Robertson, Graham	34	0	1	0	0	0	3	0	0	0	0	0	37	0	1
Di Canio, Paolo	25	1	12	2	0	0	6	0	3	2	1	0	35	2	15
Matthews, Adam	25	2	0	3	1	0	2	0	0	4	0	0	34	3	0
Colquhoun, John	25	6	4	3	0	0	1	0	1	1	1	0	30	7	5
Cassidy, Joe 1893	28	0	13	0	0	0	8	0	4	0	0	0	36	0	17
Munro, Dan	30	0	6	0	0	0	6	0	0	0	0	0	36	0	6
Templeton, Bobby	29	0	5	0	0	0	7	0	0	0	0	0	36	0	5
Moyes, Davie	19	5	0	8	1	0	0	0	0	2	1	0	29	7	0
McGinn, Niall	12	16	4	1	1	1	1	0	1	1	4	0	15	21	6
Kavanagh, Peter	32	0	5	0	0	0	3	0	0	0	0	0	35	0	5
Baillie, Lex	27	4	1	0	0	0	3	1	0	0	0	0	30	5	1
McEleny, Charlie	30	0	1	0	0	0	4	0	0	0	0	0	34	0	1
Zaluska, Lukasz	17	1	0	2	0	0	5	2	0	7	0	0	31	3	0
Gallacher, Jackie	22	0	15	10	0	10	1	0	2	0	0	0	33	0	27
McCallum, Neil	20	0	12	0	0	0	13	0	7	0	0	0	33	0	19
Byrne, Paul	24	4	4	1	1	0	1	0	0	2	0	0	28	5	4
Gravesen, Thomas	18	4	6	1	0	0	0	4	0	4	2	0	23	10	6
Gray, Stuart	19	9	1	1	0	0	1	0	0	2	1	0	23	10	1
Dunbar, Michael	15	0	4	0	0	0	17	0	6	0	0	0	32	0	10
Kiernan, Tommy	23	0	12	8	0	5	1	0	0	0	0	0	32	0	17
McPherson, Andrew	27	0	0	0	0	0	5	0	0	0	0	0	32	0	0
Crainie, Danny	17	8	7	2	4	1	0	1	0	0	0	0	19	13	8
Riordan, Derek	8	17	6	3	0	0	2	1	3	0	1	0	13	19	9
Gray, William	26	0	12	0	0	0	5	0	0	0	0	0	31	0	12
Hynds, Tom	28	0	2	0	0	0	3	0	0	0	0	0	31	0	2
McKeown, Mick	14	0	0	0	0	0	16	0	0	0	0	0	30	0	0

	LEAGUE			LG CUP			SCOT CUP			EUROPE			TOTAL		
	A	S	G	A	S	G	A	S	G	A	S	G	A	S	G
McOustra, Willie	23	0	8	0	0	0	7	0	3	0	0	0	30	0	11
Hay, Chris	9	16	4	0	0	0	0	3	0	0	2	1	9	21	5
Johnston, Leslie	24	0	8	4	0	0	1	0	0	0	0	0	29	0	8
Cascarino, Tony	13	11	4	1	0	0	0	1	0	2	1	0	16	13	4
Casey, Jim	6	7	4	4	4	0	2	1	1	3	2	0	15	14	5
Bell, Andrew	25	0	0	0	0	0	3	0	0	0	0	0	28	0	0
McAteer, Tom	24	0	4	0	0	0	4	0	1	0	0	0	28	0	5
McLean, Davie	28	0	13	0	0	0	0	0	0	0	0	0	28	0	13
Ferguson, Willie	25	0	11	0	0	0	2	0	1	0	0	0	27	0	12
Goldie, Hugh	25	0	0	0	0	0	2	0	1	0	0	0	27	0	1
Jackson, John	27	0	4	0	0	0	0	0	0	0	0	0	27	0	4
Sharkey, Jim	23	0	8	2	0	0	2	0	1	0	0	0	27	0	9
Smith, Hugh	25	0	1	0	0	0	2	0	0	0	0	0	27	0	1
Curran, John 1892	21	0	0	0	0	0	5	0	0	0	0	0	26	0	0
McAloon, Gerry	20	0	12	5	0	1	1	0	1	0	0	0	26	0	14
Millsopp, John	19	0	2	4	0	0	3	0	0	0	0	0	26	0	2
Rae, Joe	19	0	11	6	0	1	1	0	0	0	0	0	26	0	12
Vega, Ramon	18	0	2	2	0	0	6	0	2	0	0	0	26	0	4
McMillan, Duncan	18	0	0	5	0	0	2	0	0	0	0	0	25	0	0
Meehan, Peter	25	0	1	0	0	0	0	0	0	0	0	0	25	0	1
Muir, Bob	20	0	4	0	0	0	5	0	3	0	0	0	25	0	7
Pressley, Steven	19	0	1	0	0	0	4	0	1	1	1	0	24	1	2
Camara, Henri	12	5	8	0	1	0	0	1	0	4	2	0	16	9	8
Brady, Alec	19	0	4	0	0	0	5	0	6	0	0	0	24	0	10
Camara, Mo	19	0	0	3	0	0	0	0	0	2	0	0	24	0	0
Fox, Danny	15	0	0	1	0	0	0	0	0	7	1	0	23	1	0
Caddis, Paul	3	14	0	2	0	0	3	0	0	2	0	0	10	14	0
Hazlett, George	21	0	0	2	0	0	0	0	0	0	0	0	23	0	0
Livingstone, George	17	0	4	0	0	0	6	0	3	0	0	0	23	0	7

	LEAGUE			LG CUP			SCOT CUP			EUROPE			TOTAL		
	A	S	G	A	S	G	A	S	G	A	S	G	A	S	G
McFarlane, Robert	17	0	0	0	0	0	6	0	0	0	0	0	23	0	0
Bell, James	15	0	0	0	0	0	7	0	0	0	0	0	22	0	0
Pratt, David	22	0	0	0	0	0	0	0	0	0	0	0	22	0	0
Ryan, Vincent	22	0	3	0	0	0	0	0	0	0	0	0	22	0	3
Travers, Paddy	18	0	5	0	0	0	4	0	3	0	0	0	22	0	8
Munro, Frank	14	1	0	5	0	0	2	0	0	0	0	0	21	1	0
Davidson, James	21	0	10	0	0	0	0	0	0	0	0	0	21	0	10
Doyle, Frank	17	0	2	0	0	0	4	0	1	0	0	0	21	0	3
McDermott, Thomas	12	0	2	0	0	0	9	0	3	0	0	0	21	0	5
Wilson, Kelvin	13	1	0	2	0	0	3	0	0	2	0	0	20	1	0
Thompson, Josh	16	2	3	0	0	0	3	0	0	0	0	0	19	2	3
Juninho	8	5	1	2	0	0	1	1	0	2	2	0	13	8	1
Hewitt, John	9	7	0	3	2	0	0	0	0	0	0	0	12	9	0
Murphy, Daryl	9	9	3	0	1	0	0	0	0	0	2	0	9	12	3
Dawson, Daniel	17	0	3	0	0	0	3	0	0	0	0	0	20	0	3
Martin, Lee	19	0	0	1	0	0	0	0	0	0	0	0	20	0	0
O'Kane, Joe	20	0	13	0	0	0	0	0	0	0	0	0	20	0	13
Smith, Barry	14	5	0	1	0	0	0	0	0	0	0	0	15	5	0
McLaughlin, Brian '71	3	4	1	9	2	0	0	0	0	0	2	1	12	8	2
Juarez, Efrain	5	8	0	1	1	0	1	0	0	4	0	2	11	9	2
Fernandez, David	3	8	0	2	1	0	2	1	0	1	2	1	8	12	1
Allan, George	17	0	15	0	0	0	2	0	1	0	0	0	19	0	16
Fleming, William	19	0	10	0	0	0	0	0	0	0	0	0	19	0	10
Keane, Robbie	15	1	12	0	0	0	2	1	4	0	0	0	17	2	16
Cattanach, Dave	10	3	1	1	1	0	3	0	0	1	0	0	15	4	1
Zheng Zi	9	7	1	1	0	0	1	1	0	0	0	0	11	8	1
Sheridan, Cillian	6	8	4	0	1	0	0	1	0	1	2	0	7	12	4
Coleman, Johnny	7	0	2	0	0	0	11	0	0	0	0	0	18	0	2
Groves, Willie	4	0	3	0	0	0	14	0	13	0	0	0	18	0	16

	LEAGUE			LG CUP			SCOT CUP			EUROPE			TOTAL		
	A	S	G	A	S	G	A	S	G	A	S	G	A	S	G
Martin, Allan	17	0	18	0	0	0	1	0	0	0	0	0	18	0	18
McAlindon, John	16	0	7	1	0	0	1	0	0	0	0	0	18	0	7
McGuire, Jimmy	14	0	0	4	0	0	0	0	0	0	0	0	18	0	0
Sirrel, Jimmy	13	0	2	0	0	0	5	0	0	0	0	0	18	0	2
Wallace, John	15	0	0	0	0	0	3	0	0	0	0	0	18	0	0
Watson, Charlie	18	0	4	0	0	0	0	0	0	0	0	0	18	0	4
Whitelaw, Robert	17	0	0	0	0	0	1	0	0	0	0	0	18	0	0
Dowie, John	12	2	0	2	1	0	1	0	0	0	0	0	15	3	0
Crone, Willie	17	0	9	0	0	0	0	0	0	0	0	0	17	0	9
Donaldson, Andy	17	0	6	0	0	0	0	0	0	0	0	0	17	0	6
Findlay, Robert	14	0	6	0	0	0	3	0	2	0	0	0	17	0	8
McKnight, Allen	12	0	0	2	0	0	1	0	0	2	0	0	17	0	0
Baines, Roy	12	0	0	3	0	0	1	0	0	0	0	0	16	0	0
Hastie, John	16	0	3	0	0	0	0	0	1	0	0	0	16	0	4
McLaren, James	3	0	0	0	0	0	13	0	2	0	0	0	16	0	2
McMenemy, John	15	0	2	0	0	0	1	0	0	0	0	0	16	0	2
Morrison, Tommy	15	0	1	0	0	0	1	0	0	0	0	0	16	0	1
Nichol, Willie	16	0	8	0	0	0	0	0	0	0	0	0	16	0	8
Owers, Ebeneezer	13	0	8	0	0	0	3	0	1	0	0	0	16	0	9
Whittaker, Brian	10	0	2	6	0	1	0	0	0	0	0	0	16	0	3
Bellamy, Craig	12	0	7	0	0	0	3	0	2	0	0	0	15	0	9
Crossan, Barney	8	0	3	0	0	0	7	0	4	0	0	0	15	0	7
McLean, Finlay	15	0	4	0	0	0	0	0	0	0	0	0	15	0	4
Rennet, Willie	14	0	4	0	0	0	1	0	0	0	0	0	15	0	4
Halpin, John	3	4	0	1	4	0	1	1	1	0	1	0	5	10	1
Bauchop, James	14	0	5	0	0	0	0	0	0	0	0	0	14	0	5
Brown, Mark	13	0	0	0	0	0	0	0	0	1	0	0	14	0	0
Goldie, Peter	13	0	0	0	0	0	1	0	0	0	0	0	14	0	0
Gray, Alec	13	0	5	0	0	0	1	0	0	0	0	0	14	0	5

	LEAGUE A S G	LG CUP A S G	SCOT CUP A S G	EUROPE A S G	TOTAL A S G
McDonald, Pat	9 0 0	5 0 0	0 0 0	0 0 0	14 0 0
McDonald, Tommy	13 0 7	0 0 0	1 0 0	0 0 0	14 0 7
Turner, Paddy	7 0 0	6 0 0	1 0 0	0 0 0	14 0 0
Weir, John	11 0 1	2 0 0	1 0 0	0 0 0	14 0 1
Wilson, Alex	14 0 0	0 0 0	0 0 0	0 0 0	14 0 0
Anderson, Oliver	13 0 3	0 0 0	0 0 0	0 0 0	13 0 3
Burns, John	13 0 3	0 0 0	0 0 0	0 0 0	13 0 3
Connolly, Barney	13 0 4	0 0 0	0 0 0	0 0 0	13 0 4
Craig, Robert	13 0 0	0 0 0	0 0 0	0 0 0	13 0 0
Granger, John	13 0 0	0 0 0	0 0 0	0 0 0	13 0 0
Muggleton, Carl	12 0 0	0 0 0	1 0 0	0 0 0	13 0 0
Keane, Roy	10 0 1	1 1 0	1 0 0	0 0 0	12 1 1
Rasmussen, Morten	2 8 2	0 0 0	2 1 1	0 0 0	4 9 3
Fagan, Willie	12 0 9	0 0 0	0 0 0	0 0 0	12 0 9
Lochhead, Ian	7 0 2	1 0 0	4 0 1	0 0 0	12 0 3
McIlroy, James	11 0 3	1 0 0	0 0 0	0 0 0	12 0 3
Braafheid, Edson	9 1 0	0 0 0	2 0 0	0 0 0	11 1 0
Mathie, Alex	7 4 0	0 0 0	1 0 0	0 0 0	8 4 0
Dublin, Dion	3 8 1	1 0 1	0 0 0	0 0 0	4 8 2
Virgo, Adam	3 7 0	1 0 0	0 1 0	0 0 0	4 8 0
Bangura, Mohamed	2 6 0	0 1 0	0 0 0	1 2 0	3 9 0
Mizuno, Koki	2 9 1	0 1 0	0 0 0	0 0 0	2 10 1
Black, Willie	10 0 0	0 0 0	1 0 0	0 0 0	11 0 0
Callachan, Harry	11 0 0	0 0 0	0 0 0	0 0 0	11 0 0
Campbell, Robert	11 0 0	0 0 0	0 0 0	0 0 0	11 0 0
Docherty, John	11 0 0	0 0 0	0 0 0	0 0 0	11 0 0
McIlvenny, Harry	9 0 1	0 0 0	2 0 1	0 0 0	11 0 2
McIntosh, James	8 0 0	0 0 0	3 0 0	0 0 0	11 0 0
McNally, Owen	11 0 4	0 0 0	0 0 0	0 0 0	11 0 4

	LEAGUE			LG CUP			SCOT CUP			EUROPE			TOTAL		
	A	S	G	A	S	G	A	S	G	A	S	G	A	S	G
Turnbull, Tom	11	0	0	0	0	0	0	0	0	0	0	0	11	0	0
Kharine, Dimitre	7	1	0	2	0	0	0	0	0	1	0	0	10	1	0
Bone, Jimmy	5	2	1	2	1	0	1	0	0	0	0	0	8	3	1
Boyle, John	10	0	0	0	0	0	0	0	0	0	0	0	10	0	0
Boyle, Robert	10	0	0	0	0	0	0	0	0	0	0	0	10	0	0
Crawford, Alec	10	0	3	0	0	0	0	0	0	0	0	0	10	0	3
Fisher, James	10	0	3	0	0	0	0	0	0	0	0	0	10	0	3
Henderson, Adam	9	0	4	0	0	0	1	0	2	0	0	0	10	0	6
Kay, Roy	5	0	0	4	0	0	0	0	0	1	0	0	10	0	0
Kelly, John 1929	9	0	0	0	0	0	1	0	0	0	0	0	10	0	0
King, John	9	0	0	0	0	0	1	0	0	0	0	0	10	0	0
Longmuir, Archie	10	0	6	0	0	0	0	0	0	0	0	0	10	0	6
McEvoy, Pat	10	0	0	0	0	0	0	0	0	0	0	0	10	0	0
McGhee, James	10	0	4	0	0	0	0	0	0	0	0	0	10	0	4
McKay, Johnnie	10	0	6	0	0	0	0	0	0	0	0	0	10	0	6
Riley, Joseph	10	0	2	0	0	0	0	0	0	0	0	0	10	0	2
Walsh, Frank	10	0	3	0	0	0	0	0	0	0	0	0	10	0	3
Watters, Jackie	9	0	4	0	0	0	1	0	1	0	0	0	10	0	5
Hooiveld, Jos	6	1					0	0	0	3	0	0	9	1	0
Kamara, Diomansy	8	1	2	0	0	0	1	0	1	0	0	0	9	1	3
Sanchez Broto, Javier	7	1	0	0	0	0	2	0	0	0	0	0	9	1	0
Hayes, Martin	3	4	0	3	0	0	0	0	0	0	0	0	6	4	0
Ritchie, Andy	5	4	1	0	1	1	0	0	0	0	0	0	5	5	2
Biggins, Wayne	4	5	0	0	0	0	0	1	0	0	0	0	4	6	0
Gray, Michael	2	5	0	1	0	0	0	0	0	1	1	0	4	6	0
Boyle, James	9	0	0	0	0	0	0	0	0	0	0	0	9	0	0
Cantwell, Jack	8	0	5	1	0	0	0	0	0	0	0	0	9	0	5
Craig, Billy	8	0	0	0	0	0	1	0	0	0	0	0	9	0	0
Craig, Tully	9	0	3	0	0	0	0	0	0	0	0	0	9	0	3

	LEAGUE			LG CUP			SCOT CUP			EUROPE			TOTAL		
	A	S	G	A	S	G	A	S	G	A	S	G	A	S	G
Docherty, Tommy	9	0	3	0	0	0	0	0	0	0	0	0	9	0	3
Duff, Tom	8	0	0	0	0	0	1	0	0	0	0	0	9	0	0
Duncan, James	8	0	2	1	0	0	0	0	0	0	0	0	9	0	2
Duncan, Willie	9	0	0	0	0	0	0	0	0	0	0	0	9	0	0
Dunn, Willie	9	0	2	0	0	0	0	0	0	0	0	0	9	0	2
Kurila, John	5	0	0	4	0	0	0	0	0	0	0	0	9	0	0
Maley, Tom	2	0	0	0	0	0	7	0	0	0	0	0	9	0	0
McInally, John	9	0	5	0	0	0	0	0	0	0	0	0	9	0	5
Millar, Alex	9	0	0	0	0	0	0	0	0	0	0	0	9	0	0
O'Hara, Dan	7	0	1	0	0	0	2	0	0	0	0	0	9	0	1
O'Rourke, Peter	9	0	0	0	0	0	0	0	0	0	0	0	9	0	0
Quinn, Robert	6	0	0	3	0	0	0	0	0	0	0	0	9	0	0
Solis, Jerome	9	0	3	0	0	0	0	0	0	0	0	0	9	0	3
Whyte, Frank	7	0	0	2	0	0	0	0	0	0	0	0	9	0	0
McCahill, Steve	6	1	0	1	0	0	1	0	0	0	0	0	8	1	0
Wright, Ian	4	4	3	1	0	0	0	0	0	0	0	0	5	4	3
Flood, Willo	2	4	0	1	0	0	0	0	0	1	1	0	4	5	0
Andrews, Ian	5	0	0	2	0	0	0	0	0	1	0	0	8	0	0
Connor, Frank	2	0	0	6	0	0	0	0	0	0	0	0	8	0	0
Conroy, Mike 1953	7	0	0	1	0	0	0	0	0	0	0	0	8	0	0
Cunningham, Johnny	7	0	0	0	0	0	1	0	0	0	0	0	8	0	0
Falconer, John	7	0	0	0	0	0	1	0	0	0	0	0	8	0	0
Jeffrey, Bobby	5	0	0	3	0	0	0	0	0	0	0	0	8	0	0
Kapler, Konrad	7	0	0	1	0	0	0	0	0	0	0	0	8	0	0
Malloy, Willie	7	0	1	0	0	0	1	0	0	0	0	0	8	0	1
Maxwell, Hugh	8	0	0	0	0	0	0	0	0	0	0	0	8	0	0
Semple, Willie	8	0	2	0	0	0	0	0	0	0	0	0	8	0	2
Perrier-Doumbe JJ	5	1	0	0	0	0	1	0	1	1	0	0	7	1	1
Smith, Mark	3	3	0	2	0	0	0	0	0	0	0	0	5	3	0

	LEAGUE			LG CUP			SCOT CUP			EUROPE			TOTAL		
	A	S	G	A	S	G	A	S	G	A	S	G	A	S	G
Henchoz, Stephane	2	4	0	0	0	0	2	0	0	0	0	0	4	4	0
McGowan, Paul	2	4	0	0	0	0	0	0	0	1	1	1	3	5	1
Ljungberg, Freddie	1	6	0	0	0	0	1	0	0	0	0	0	2	6	0
McGeouch, Dylan	1	5	1	0	0	0	0	2	0	0	0	0	1	7	1
Hammill, Micky	7	0	0	0	0	0	0	0	0	0	0	0	7	0	0
Jarvis, George	7	0	0	0	0	0	0	0	0	0	0	0	7	0	0
Lafferty, James	7	0	4	0	0	0	0	0	0	0	0	0	7	0	4
McCann, Dan	7	0	1	0	0	0	0	0	0	0	0	0	7	0	1
McWilliam, Bobby	7	0	0	0	0	0	0	0	0	0	0	0	7	0	0
Murphy, James F	6	0	2	0	0	0	1	0	0	0	0	0	7	0	2
O'Byrne, Fergus	7	0	0	0	0	0	0	0	0	0	0	0	7	0	0
Orr, Jim	7	0	0	0	0	0	0	0	0	0	0	0	7	0	0
Quinn, Frankie	6	0	0	1	0	0	0	0	0	0	0	0	7	0	0
Rough, Alan	5	0	0	1	0	0	0	0	0	1	0	0	7	0	0
Tierney, Con	7	0	0	0	0	0	0	0	0	0	0	0	7	0	0
Weir, Donald	6	0	1	0	0	0	1	0	1	0	0	0	7	0	2
Whitehead, George	7	0	2	0	0	0	0	0	0	0	0	0	7	0	2
El Kaddouri, Badr	5	1	1	1	0	0	0	0	0	0	0	0	6	1	1
Dobbin, Jim	1	2	0	4	0	1	0	0	0	0	0	0	5	2	1
Airlie, Seton	6	0	3	0	0	0	0	0	0	0	0	0	6	0	3
Birrell, Jimmy	6	0	2	0	0	0	0	0	0	0	0	0	6	0	2
Davidson, Andrew	5	0	0	0	0	0	1	0	0	0	0	0	6	0	0
Dunning, Willie	0	0	0	0	0	0	6	0	0	0	0	0	6	0	0
Foley, James	6	0	0	0	0	0	0	0	0	0	0	0	6	0	0
Garry, Edward	6	0	1	0	0	0	0	0	0	0	0	0	6	0	1
Hepburn, Anthony	6	0	0	0	0	0	0	0	0	0	0	0	6	0	0
Leitch, William	5	0	1	0	0	0	1	0	0	0	0	0	6	0	1
McGhee, Joe	5	0	2	0	0	0	1	0	0	0	0	0	6	0	2
McGrogan, Vincent	5	0	0	0	0	0	1	0	0	0	0	0	6	0	0

	LEAGUE A S G			LG CUP A S G			SCOT CUP A S G			EUROPE A S G			TOTAL A S G		
Prentice, David	6	0	1	0	0	0	0	0	0	0	0	0	6	0	1
Sinclair, Tom 1906	6	0	0	0	0	0	0	0	0	0	0	0	6	0	0
McMahon, Pat	2	1	2	3	0	3	0	0	0	0	0	0	5	1	5
Elliot, David	2	4	0	0	0	0	0	0	0	0	0	0	2	4	0
Mackie, Peter	1	3	0	1	1	0	0	0	0	0	0	0	2	4	0
Scheidt, Rafael	1	3	0	0	0	0	0	0	0	1	1	0	2	4	0
Hutchison, Ben	0	5	0	0	0	0	0	0	0	0	1	0	0	6	0
Barber, Tom	5	0	0	0	0	0	0	0	0	0	0	0	5	0	0
Clifford, Hugh	5	0	0	0	0	0	0	0	0	0	0	0	5	0	0
Donnelly, Willie	3	0	0	0	0	0	2	0	0	0	0	0	5	0	0
Doyle, Tom	5	0	0	0	0	0	0	0	0	0	0	0	5	0	0
Ferguson, George	5	0	0	0	0	0	0	0	0	0	0	0	5	0	0
Fitzsimmons, John	5	0	0	0	0	0	0	0	0	0	0	0	5	0	0
Heron, Gil	1	0	0	4	0	2	0	0	0	0	0	0	5	0	2
Hughes, John 1922	5	0	0	0	0	0	0	0	0	0	0	0	5	0	0
Mackle, Tommy	3	0	1	2	0	1	0	0	0	0	0	0	5	0	2
Miller, Andrew	5	0	1	0	0	0	0	0	0	0	0	0	5	0	1
Mitchell, William	5	0	0	0	0	0	0	0	0	0	0	0	5	0	0
O'Neill, Hugh	5	0	0	0	0	0	0	0	0	0	0	0	5	0	0
Slater, Malcolm	5	0	1	0	0	0	0	0	0	0	0	0	5	0	1
Taylor, David	5	0	0	0	0	0	0	0	0	0	0	0	5	0	0
Towie, Tom	0	0	0	0	0	0	5	0	2	0	0	0	5	0	2
Ugolini, Rolando	4	0	0	1	0	0	0	0	0	0	0	0	5	0	0
Walls, James	4	0	0	0	0	0	1	0	0	0	0	0	5	0	0
Lustig, Mikael	3	1	0	0	0	0	1	0	0	0	0	0	4	1	0
McLaughlin, Paul	2	1	0	2	0	0	0	0	0	0	0	0	4	1	0
McQuilken, Jamie	4	1	0	0	0	0	0	0	0	0	0	0	4	1	0
Welsh, Frank	4	1	0	0	0	0	0	0	0	0	0	0	4	1	0
Lynch, Simon	2	1	3	0	0	0	0	0	0	1	1	0	3	2	3

	LEAGUE A	S	G	LG CUP A	S	G	SCOT CUP A	S	G	EUROPE A	S	G	TOTAL A	S	G
Black, John	4	0	1	0	0	0	0	0	0	0	0	0	4	0	1
Cairney, James	3	0	0	0	0	0	1	0	0	0	0	0	4	0	0
Cameron, James	4	0	2	0	0	0	0	0	0	0	0	0	4	0	2
Connor, John	4	0	1	0	0	0	0	0	0	0	0	0	4	0	1
Corrigan, Edward	4	0	0	0	0	0	0	0	0	0	0	0	4	0	0
Curran, John 1958	4	0	0	0	0	0	0	0	0	0	0	0	4	0	0
Doherty, Hugh	3	0	0	0	0	0	1	0	0	0	0	0	4	0	0
Dolan, Michael	3	0	0	0	0	0	1	0	0	0	0	0	4	0	0
Drummond, James	4	0	1	0	0	0	0	0	0	0	0	0	4	0	1
Duffy, Robert	4	0	0	0	0	0	0	0	0	0	0	0	4	0	0
Flannagan, M	4	0	1	0	0	0	0	0	0	0	0	0	4	0	1
Graham, John	4	0	0	0	0	0	0	0	0	0	0	0	4	0	0
Hemple, Sam	4	0	2	0	0	0	0	0	0	0	0	0	4	0	2
Henderson, John	3	0	0	0	0	0	1	0	0	0	0	0	4	0	0
Lavery, Dan	4	0	1	0	0	0	0	0	0	0	0	0	4	0	1
Lees, Walter	4	0	3	0	0	0	0	0	0	0	0	0	4	0	3
McGillivray, Charlie	4	0	2	0	0	0	0	0	0	0	0	0	4	0	2
Mulvey, Mick	4	0	4	0	0	0	0	0	0	0	0	0	4	0	4
O'Sullivan, Pat	4	0	0	0	0	0	0	0	0	0	0	0	4	0	0
Reid, Ian	4	0	1	0	0	0	0	0	0	0	0	0	4	0	1
Reynolds, Jack	4	0	1	0	0	0	0	0	0	0	0	0	4	0	1
Robertson, William	3	0	0	0	0	0	1	0	0	0	0	0	4	0	0
Whitney, Tom	4	0	1	0	0	0	0	0	0	0	0	0	4	0	1
McWilliams, Ian	1	0	0	1	1	0	0	0	0	1	0	0	3	1	0
Traynor, John	3	1	0	0	0	0	0	0	0	0	0	0	3	1	0
Gibson, Johnny	1	2	0	0	0	0	0	1	0	0	0	0	1	3	0
Lawson, Paul	1	2	0	0	1	0	0	0	0	0	0	0	1	3	0
McBride, John Paul	1	2	0	0	0	0	0	0	0	0	1	0	1	3	0
McCarrison, Dugald	1	3	0	0	0	0	0	0	0	0	0	0	1	3	0

	LEAGUE			LG CUP			SCOT CUP			EUROPE			TOTAL		
	A	S	G	A	S	G	A	S	G	A	S	G	A	S	G
Britton, Gerry	0	2	0	0	0	0	0	2	0	0	0	0	0	4	0
Chalmers, Paul	0	4	1	0	0	0	0	0	0	0	0	0	0	4	1
McGuire, Dougie	0	2	0	0	1	0	0	0	0	0	1	0	0	4	0
Blair, Dan	3	0	0	0	0	0	0	0	0	0	0	0	3	0	0
Cannon, Bernard	3	0	0	0	0	0	0	0	0	0	0	0	3	0	0
Coen, Joseph	3	0	0	0	0	0	0	0	0	0	0	0	3	0	0
Corcoran, Patrick	3	0	0	0	0	0	0	0	0	0	0	0	3	0	0
Crilly, Willie	3	0	0	0	0	0	0	0	0	0	0	0	3	0	0
Devanny, Alex	1	0	0	2	0	0	0	0	0	0	0	0	3	0	0
Garner, Willie	1	0	0	2	0	0	0	0	0	0	0	0	3	0	0
Gilgun, Paddy	3	0	1	0	0	0	0	0	0	0	0	0	3	0	1
Jordan, Jackie	3	0	1	0	0	0	0	0	0	0	0	0	3	0	1
Kelly, Johnny 1960	3	0	0	0	0	0	0	0	0	0	0	0	3	0	0
Lawrie, Willie	3	0	0	0	0	0	0	0	0	0	0	0	3	0	0
McCallum, Willie	1	0	0	0	0	0	2	0	0	0	0	0	3	0	0
McCann, John	3	0	0	0	0	0	0	0	0	0	0	0	3	0	0
McCann, William	3	0	0	0	0	0	0	0	0	0	0	0	3	0	0
McDonald, Willie	3	0	0	0	0	0	0	0	0	0	0	0	3	0	0
McLaughlin, James '88	0	0	0	0	0	0	3	0	0	0	0	0	3	0	0
McLean, Lachlan	3	0	0	0	0	0	0	0	0	0	0	0	3	0	0
Moran, Martin	3	0	0	0	0	0	0	0	0	0	0	0	3	0	0
Shevlane, Chris	2	0	0	1	0	0	0	0	0	0	0	0	3	0	0
Shields, Jimmy	3	0	0	0	0	0	0	0	0	0	0	0	3	0	0
Slavin, Jim	3	0	0	0	0	0	0	0	0	0	0	0	3	0	0
Warner, Tony	3	0	0	0	0	0	0	0	0	0	0	0	3	0	0
Watson, Phil	3	0	0	0	0	0	0	0	0	0	0	0	3	0	0
Young, John	3	0	0	0	0	0	0	0	0	0	0	0	3	0	0
Conroy, Ryan	2	0	0	0	0	0	0	1	0	0	0	0	2	1	0
Fotheringham, Mark	2	1	0	0	0	0	0	0	0	0	0	0	2	1	0

	LEAGUE			LG CUP			SCOT CUP			EUROPE			TOTAL		
	A	S	G	A	S	G	A	S	G	A	S	G	A	S	G
Gray, John	2	1	0	0	0	0	0	0	0	0	0	0	2	1	0
McInally, Jim	0	1	0	1	0	0	1	0	0	0	0	0	2	1	0
Blackman, Andre	1	2	0	0	0	0	0	0	0	0	0	0	1	2	0
Brozek, Pawel	1	2	0	0	0	0	0	0	0	0	0	0	1	2	0
Anthony, Marc	0	2	0	0	1	0	0	0	0	0	0	0	0	3	0
Twardzik, Filip	0	1	0	0	0	0	0	2	0	0	0	0	0	3	0
Watt, Tony	0	3	2	0	0	0	0	0	0	0	0	0	0	3	2
Allan, Thomas	2	0	0	0	0	0	0	0	0	0	0	0	2	0	0
Brodie, John	2	0	1	0	0	0	0	0	0	0	0	0	2	0	1
Clark, Joe	2	0	0	0	0	0	0	0	0	0	0	0	2	0	0
Clark, John 1903	2	0	0	0	0	0	0	0	0	0	0	0	2	0	0
Collins, Alec	0	0	0	0	0	0	2	0	0	0	0	0	2	0	0
Collins, Frank	2	0	0	0	0	0	0	0	0	0	0	0	2	0	0
Crozier, James	2	0	0	0	0	0	0	0	0	0	0	0	2	0	0
Devlin, James	2	0	0	0	0	0	0	0	0	0	0	0	2	0	0
Devlin, John	2	0	1	0	0	0	0	0	0	0	0	0	2	0	1
Docherty, James 1954	1	0	0	1	0	0	0	0	0	0	0	0	2	0	0
Docherty, Jim 1947	2	0	0	0	0	0	0	0	0	0	0	0	2	0	0
Doherty, John	2	0	0	0	0	0	0	0	0	0	0	0	2	0	0
Dolan, Frank	2	0	0	0	0	0	0	0	0	0	0	0	2	0	0
Duffy, John	2	0	0	0	0	0	0	0	0	0	0	0	2	0	0
Duncan, Scott	2	0	0	0	0	0	0	0	0	0	0	0	2	0	0
Foran, Joseph	2	0	1	0	0	0	0	0	0	0	0	0	2	0	1
Gallagher, Antony	2	0	1	0	0	0	0	0	0	0	0	0	2	0	1
Gallagher, Jimmy	2	0	0	0	0	0	0	0	0	0	0	0	2	0	0
Gallagher, Pat	2	0	0	0	0	0	0	0	0	0	0	0	2	0	0
Geddes, John	2	0	0	0	0	0	0	0	0	0	0	0	2	0	0
Gibson, Andrew	2	0	1	0	0	0	0	0	0	0	0	0	2	0	1
Gilfeather, Eddie	2	0	0	0	0	0	0	0	0	0	0	0	2	0	0

	LEAGUE			LG CUP			SCOT CUP			EUROPE			TOTAL		
	A	S	G	A	S	G	A	S	G	A	S	G	A	S	G
Gilligan, Sam	2	0	0	0	0	0	0	0	0	0	0	0	2	0	0
Glasgow, Sam	2	0	0	0	0	0	0	0	0	0	0	0	2	0	0
Grassam, Willie	2	0	0	0	0	0	0	0	0	0	0	0	2	0	0
Healy, James	2	0	0	0	0	0	0	0	0	0	0	0	2	0	0
Henderson, Sam	2	0	0	0	0	0	0	0	0	0	0	0	2	0	0
Hill, John	2	0	0	0	0	0	0	0	0	0	0	0	2	0	0
Hutchison, Tom	2	0	0	0	0	0	0	0	0	0	0	0	2	0	0
Kelly, Charlie	2	0	0	0	0	0	0	0	0	0	0	0	2	0	0
Kelly, Frank	2	0	0	0	0	0	0	0	0	0	0	0	2	0	0
Kelly, John 1888	0	0	0	0	0	0	2	0	0	0	0	0	2	0	0
Kyle, James	2	0	0	0	0	0	0	0	0	0	0	0	2	0	0
Lynch, Allan	2	0	0	0	0	0	0	0	0	0	0	0	2	0	0
McCabe, Pat	2	0	0	0	0	0	0	0	0	0	0	0	2	0	0
McColgan, Dan	2	0	0	0	0	0	0	0	0	0	0	0	2	0	0
McCormack, Harry	2	0	1	0	0	0	0	0	0	0	0	0	2	0	1
McDonald, John	0	0	0	2	0	2	0	0	0	0	0	0	2	0	2
McElhaney, Ralph	2	0	0	0	0	0	0	0	0	0	0	0	2	0	0
McGinn, James	2	0	0	0	0	0	0	0	0	0	0	0	2	0	0
McLaughlin, Jim	2	0	0	0	0	0	0	0	0	0	0	0	2	0	0
McMillan, Thomas	0	0	0	2	0	0	0	0	0	0	0	0	2	0	0
McNeil, Hugh	2	0	0	0	0	0	0	0	0	0	0	0	2	0	0
Murray, Michael	2	0	0	0	0	0	0	0	0	0	0	0	2	0	0
O'Connor, John	1	0	0	0	0	0	1	0	0	0	0	0	2	0	0
Oliver, Jim	2	0	0	0	0	0	0	0	0	0	0	0	2	0	0
Ribchester, Willie	2	0	0	0	0	0	0	0	0	0	0	0	2	0	0
Robertson, David	2	0	0	0	0	0	0	0	0	0	0	0	2	0	0
Rowan, Jim	2	0	1	0	0	0	0	0	0	0	0	0	2	0	1
Sanderson, Robert	2	0	0	0	0	0	0	0	0	0	0	0	2	0	0
Sinclair, Tommy 1927	2	0	0	0	0	0	0	0	0	0	0	0	2	0	0

	LEAGUE			LG CUP			SCOT CUP			EUROPE			TOTAL		
	A	S	G	A	S	G	A	S	G	A	S	G	A	S	G
Strang, William	2	0	0	0	0	0	0	0	0	0	0	0	2	0	0
Syme, David	2	0	0	0	0	0	0	0	0	0	0	0	2	0	0
Toner, Willie	2	0	0	0	0	0	0	0	0	0	0	0	2	0	0
Turnbull, David	2	0	0	0	0	0	0	0	0	0	0	0	2	0	0
Coyle, Ronnie	1	1	0	0	0	0	0	0	0	0	0	0	1	1	0
Henderson, Athol	0	0	0	1	1	0	0	0	0	0	0	0	1	1	0
Kapo, Olivier	1	1	0	0	0	0	0	0	0	0	0	0	1	1	0
Marshall, Scott	1	1	0	0	0	0	0	0	0	0	0	0	1	1	0
McKechnie, Jim	1	1	0	0	0	0	0	0	0	0	0	0	1	1	0
Aliadiere, Jeremie	0	0	0	0	0	0	0	0	0	0	2	0	0	2	0
De Ornales, Fernando	0	2	0	0	0	0	0	0	0	0	0	0	0	2	0
Hannah, Robert	0	2	0	0	0	0	0	0	0	0	0	0	0	2	0
O'Brien, Jim	0	1	0	0	0	0	0	1	0	0	0	0	0	2	0
Arnott, Walker	1	0	0	0	0	0	0	0	0	0	0	0	1	0	0
Atkinson, John	1	0	0	0	0	0	0	0	0	0	0	0	1	0	0
Barclay, Graham	0	0	0	0	0	0	1	0	0	0	0	0	1	0	0
Barrie, Jim	1	0	0	0	0	0	0	0	0	0	0	0	1	0	0
Bjarnason, Teddy	1	0	0	0	0	0	0	0	0	0	0	0	1	0	0
Blackwood, John	1	0	0	0	0	0	0	0	0	0	0	0	1	0	0
Blair, John	1	0	0	0	0	0	0	0	0	0	0	0	1	0	0
Breslin, Pat	1	0	0	0	0	0	0	0	0	0	0	0	1	0	0
Buckley, John	0	0	0	1	0	0	0	0	0	0	0	0	1	0	0
Cairney, Charles	1	0	0	0	0	0	0	0	0	0	0	0	1	0	0
Carlin, James	1	0	0	0	0	0	0	0	0	0	0	0	1	0	0
Cassidy, Jimmy	1	0	0	0	0	0	0	0	0	0	0	0	1	0	0
Coleman, James	1	0	0	0	0	0	0	0	0	0	0	0	1	0	0
Connachan, James	1	0	0	0	0	0	0	0	0	0	0	0	1	0	0
Cowan, Joseph	1	0	1	0	0	0	0	0	0	0	0	0	1	0	1
Curley, Tom	1	0	0	0	0	0	0	0	0	0	0	0	1	0	0

	LEAGUE			LG CUP			SCOT CUP			EUROPE			TOTAL		
---	A	S	G	A	S	G	A	S	G	A	S	G	A	S	G
Davitt, Michael	1	0	0	0	0	0	0	0	0	0	0	0	1	0	0
Donlevey, Pat	1	0	0	0	0	0	0	0	0	0	0	0	1	0	0
Du Wei	0	0	0	0	0	0	1	0	0	0	0	0	1	0	0
Elliott, George	1	0	0	0	0	0	0	0	0	0	0	0	1	0	0
Farrell, Paddy	1	0	0	0	0	0	0	0	0	0	0	0	1	0	0
Ferguson, John	1	0	1	0	0	0	0	0	0	0	0	0	1	0	1
Fitzsimmons, Tom	1	0	0	0	0	0	0	0	0	0	0	0	1	0	0
Fraser, Bert	1	0	0	0	0	0	0	0	0	0	0	0	1	0	0
Fullarton, Alex	1	0	0	0	0	0	0	0	0	0	0	0	1	0	0
Gallagher, Hugh	1	0	1	0	0	0	0	0	0	0	0	0	1	0	1
Garden, William	1	0	0	0	0	0	0	0	0	0	0	0	1	0	0
Geehrin, Pat	1	0	0	0	0	0	0	0	0	0	0	0	1	0	0
Glancey, Lawrence	1	0	0	0	0	0	0	0	0	0	0	0	1	0	0
Goldie, Willie	1	0	0	0	0	0	0	0	0	0	0	0	1	0	0
Goodwin, Jim	1	0	0	0	0	0	0	0	0	0	0	0	1	0	0
Gorman, John	0	0	0	1	0	0	0	0	0	0	0	0	1	0	0
Gormley, Phil	1	0	0	0	0	0	0	0	0	0	0	0	1	0	0
Haverty, Joe	1	0	0	0	0	0	0	0	0	0	0	0	1	0	0
Jack, Peter	1	0	0	0	0	0	0	0	0	0	0	0	1	0	0
Kelly, John 1938	1	0	0	0	0	0	0	0	0	0	0	0	1	0	0
Kelly, John 1939	1	0	0	0	0	0	0	0	0	0	0	0	1	0	0
Kelly, Paddy	1	0	0	0	0	0	0	0	0	0	0	0	1	0	0
Kennedy, John 1965	0	0	0	1	0	0	0	0	0	0	0	0	1	0	0
Lamb, Peter	1	0	0	0	0	0	0	0	0	0	0	0	1	0	0
Madden, Dick	1	0	0	0	0	0	0	0	0	0	0	0	1	0	0
Mair, Matt	1	0	0	0	0	0	0	0	0	0	0	0	1	0	0
Marshall, Gordon '71	0	0	0	0	0	0	0	0	0	1	0	0	1	0	0
McArdle, John	1	0	0	0	0	0	0	0	0	0	0	0	1	0	0
McAulay, Willie	1	0	1	0	0	0	0	0	0	0	0	0	1	0	1

	LEAGUE			LG CUP			SCOT CUP			EUROPE			TOTAL		
	A	S	G	A	S	G	A	S	G	A	S	G	A	S	G
McCafferty, Willie	1	0	0	0	0	0	0	0	0	0	0	0	1	0	0
McCann, Eddie	1	0	0	0	0	0	0	0	0	0	0	0	1	0	0
McCann, Ryan	1	0	0	0	0	0	0	0	0	0	0	0	1	0	0
McCarron, Frank	1	0	0	0	0	0	0	0	0	0	0	0	1	0	0
McColligan, Brian	1	0	0	0	0	0	0	0	0	0	0	0	1	0	0
McCondichie, Andy	1	0	0	0	0	0	0	0	0	0	0	0	1	0	0
McCormack, Arthur	1	0	0	0	0	0	0	0	0	0	0	0	1	0	0
McCreadie, Bernard	1	0	0	0	0	0	0	0	0	0	0	0	1	0	0
McDowall, Daniel	1	0	0	0	0	0	0	0	0	0	0	0	1	0	0
McGee, Robert	1	0	0	0	0	0	0	0	0	0	0	0	1	0	0
McGinnigle, Willie	1	0	0	0	0	0	0	0	0	0	0	0	1	0	0
McGregor, Alec	1	0	0	0	0	0	0	0	0	0	0	0	1	0	0
McInally, Arthur	1	0	0	0	0	0	0	0	0	0	0	0	1	0	0
McLaughlin, ?	1	0	0	0	0	0	0	0	0	0	0	0	1	0	0
McLaughlin, George	1	0	0	0	0	0	0	0	0	0	0	0	1	0	0
McMahon, Eamon	1	0	0	0	0	0	0	0	0	0	0	0	1	0	0
McManus, Peter	1	0	0	0	0	0	0	0	0	0	0	0	1	0	0
McNair, Willie	1	0	0	0	0	0	0	0	0	0	0	0	1	0	0
McPherson, James	0	0	0	0	0	0	1	0	0	0	0	0	1	0	0
Mills, Hugh	1	0	0	0	0	0	0	0	0	0	0	0	1	0	0
Mitchell, Ronald	1	0	0	0	0	0	0	0	0	0	0	0	1	0	0
Morrison, Alex	1	0	0	0	0	0	0	0	0	0	0	0	1	0	0
Morrison, William	1	0	0	0	0	0	0	0	0	0	0	0	1	0	0
Nelson, John	1	0	0	0	0	0	0	0	0	0	0	0	1	0	0
Nicol, Davie	1	0	0	0	0	0	0	0	0	0	0	0	1	0	0
O'Brien, John	1	0	0	0	0	0	0	0	0	0	0	0	1	0	0
O'Neill, Felix	1	0	0	0	0	0	0	0	0	0	0	0	1	0	0
Paton, Roy	0	0	0	0	0	0	1	0	0	0	0	0	1	0	0
Power, Pat	1	0	0	0	0	0	0	0	0	0	0	0	1	0	0

	LEAGUE			LG CUP			SCOT CUP			EUROPE			TOTAL		
	A	S	G	A	S	G	A	S	G	A	S	G	A	S	G
Roose, Leigh	0	0	0	0	0	0	1	0	0	0	0	0	1	0	0
Ross, Andrew	1	0	0	0	0	0	0	0	0	0	0	0	1	0	0
Scott, Robert	1	0	0	0	0	0	0	0	0	0	0	0	1	0	0
Shaw, Hugh	1	0	0	0	0	0	0	0	0	0	0	0	1	0	0
Shea, Danny	1	0	0	0	0	0	0	0	0	0	0	0	1	0	0
Slaven, Pat	1	0	0	0	0	0	0	0	0	0	0	0	1	0	0
Stewart, Tom	1	0	0	0	0	0	0	0	0	0	0	0	1	0	0
Taylor, William	1	0	0	0	0	0	0	0	0	0	0	0	1	0	0
Thom, James	1	0	0	0	0	0	0	0	0	0	0	0	1	0	0
Thomas, Danny	1	0	0	0	0	0	0	0	0	0	0	0	1	0	0
Thomson, William	1	0	0	0	0	0	0	0	0	0	0	0	1	0	0
Trodden, Paddy	1	0	0	0	0	0	0	0	0	0	0	0	1	0	0
Wraith, Bobby	0	0	0	1	0	0	0	0	0	0	0	0	1	0	0
Young, James 1918	1	0	0	0	0	0	0	0	0	0	0	0	1	0	0
Carey, Graham	0	0	0	0	0	0	0	0	0	0	0	0	0	1	0
Convery, John	0	1	0	0	0	0	0	0	0	0	0	0	0	1	0
Corr, Barry J	0	1	0	0	0	0	0	0	0	0	0	0	0	1	0
Coyne, Brian	0	1	0	0	0	0	0	0	0	0	0	0	0	1	0
Craig, Michael	0	0	0	0	0	0	0	1	0	0	0	0	0	1	0
Elliot, Barry	0	1	0	0	0	0	0	0	0	0	0	0	0	1	0
Fraser, Marcus	0	0	0	0	0	0	0	0	0	0	1	0	0	1	0
Hancock, Steve	0	0	0	0	0	0	0	0	0	0	1	0	0	1	0
Ibrahim, Rabiu	0	1	0	0	0	0	0	0	0	0	0	0	0	1	0
McCluskey, John	0	0	0	0	0	0	0	0	0	0	1	0	0	1	0
McGlinchey, Michael	0	1	0	0	0	0	0	0	0	0	0	0	0	1	0
O'Neill, John	0	1	0	0	0	0	0	0	0	0	0	0	0	1	0
Paul, George	0	0	0	0	1	0	0	0	0	0	0	0	0	1	0
Shields, Paul	0	1	0	0	0	0	0	0	0	0	0	0	0	1	0
Toshney, Lewis	0	1	0	0	0	0	0	0	0	0	0	0	0	1	0
Towell, Richie	0	1	0	0	0	0	0	0	0	0	0	0	0	1	0

CELTIC FC
INFORMATION

THE CELTIC FOUNDATION

THE Celtic Foundation continues to support the Club's social dimension linked to the reasons Brother Walfrid founded Celtic FC back in 1887.

The progress made over the past few years has been significant.

The support of everyone at Celtic, dedicated staff, our partners and our client groups makes this work something unique, something which will be valued by participants for years to come.

The club is delighted to have the support of Billy Connolly as Patron of the Celtic Foundation and Elaine C Smith is the Patron on the Celtic women's and girls' programme.

The Celtic Foundation continues to integrate a number of very successful project areas with new business ideas and incorporates the following key strands:

• **Celtic Charity Fund**

• **Celtic learning programmes and the Celtic Learning Centre**

• **Football in the community and community coaching programmes in both domestic and international markets**

• **A Community Academy aimed at children, youths and adults**

• **Celtic girls' community programme and Girls' Academy**

• **Celtic women's First Team and Reserves**

• **'Sport for Life' programmes**

In addition the Foundation has a number of specialist projects which focus on:

• **Health and wellbeing**

• **Education**

• **Social Inclusion**

• **Unemployment**

This structure and work is indicative of the importance Celtic attaches to its role in the community.

The Celtic Foundation reinforces that role and the responsibility the club attaches to working alongside key partners to deliver key policy set by local and central government.

The acknowledgement and endorsements made by our partners is testimony to the work the Foundation is doing.

The 'Ability Counts' programme is the most recent Foundation innovative project in partnership with Down's Syndrome Scotland and the first of its kind in the country.

The programme covers and delivers the following for children and young people with Down's Syndrome:

• **Promotes friendships between the children and young people through a common goal and interest**

• **Engages children and young people with Down's Syndrome**

• **Promotes health and wellbeing**

- Uses football as a positive engagement tool

- Improves fitness levels

- Improves confidence and self-esteem

- Increases social skills through learning about and developing team work

- Promotes inclusion in football

- Celebrates difference and diversity

The programme has been a huge success, with excellent feedback from parents, participants and Down's Syndrome Scotland.

All the children involved have demonstrated an improved understanding of healthy lifestyle choices, fitness and flexibility, confidence and self-esteem, team-working, communication and additionally have increased their core football skills.

The children have also visited Celtic's training facility in Lennoxtown and had an opportunity to put their skills to the test against the first team management and first team players.

They also had the 'once-in-a-lifetime' experience of going on to the pitch at half-time in front of 60,000 supporters at a match at Celtic Park.

Patron of the Celtic Foundation Billy Connolly

CELTIC CHARITY FUND

Celtic Charity Fund was formed in 1995 and operates as a charitable trust, aiming to uphold and promote the charitable principles and heritage of Celtic Football Club through raising funds and supporting specific areas of charity work.

Since inception, the Fund has raised over £3m to support charities in Scotland, Ireland and across the globe on behalf of the glorious Celtic family.

How is the money raised?

There are various activities throughout the year including the Annual Sporting Dinner, Club Couture Fashion Show, Matchday Collection, Abseil or other sponsored event, Celtic Charity Cup 5-a-side Football Tournament and, on occasion, a charity football match and shirt auction. We also have a source of invaluable income through regular Standing Orders and one-off donations. In May 2010, we released a charity version of fans' favourite, *'Just Can't Get Enough'* in memory of Reamonn Gormley, to support the Good Child Foundation in Thailand and Crimestoppers Scotland's work on knife crime.

How is the money distributed?

We have an application process in place - with two closing dates per year: June 30 and December 31 - but continue to receive bids totalling far greater than the funds we have available. The three Trustees make decisions based primarily on each application's alignment with our

principal and subsidiary areas of support:-

Principal

- Charities in support of children's needs

Community action on drugs

- Projects that develop and promote religious and ethnic harmony

Subsidiary

- Supporting the homeless

- Helping the unemployed

- Support and research for projects aiding the afflictions of illness, famine and innocent families within areas of war

With some fundraising events, we also nominate a Main Beneficiary and, in 2010/11, these included Teenage Cancer Trust, Breast Cancer Care Scotland, ChildLine Scotland and Children's Hospice Association Scotland (CHAS). In addition, we do our very best to respond to international disasters and, in the last few years, made donations to the Haiti Earthquake Appeal, Australian Bushfires and Flood Appeals and Oxfam's Japan Appeal.

Why should I get involved?

It is **OUR** Charity Fund – the whole of the Celtic Family – from the owners of the club to management to players to coaches to staff to supporters to

*Victor Wanyama was one of the Celtic first-team
involved in the 2011/12 Club Couture Fashion Show*

sponsors to partners so everyone should be given the opportunity to get involved and take more ownership of it. Individual charitable donations, without doubt, make a genuine difference but, if we pool our resources and make cumulative contributions on behalf of the Celtic Family, together we can generate a huge impact. We have a formidable and much admired reputation for helping those less fortunate and our identity is highly respected worldwide. Your invaluable support is helping us continue this vital work and it's genuinely appreciated.

Further information on Celtic Charity Fund and our activities can be found at **www.celticfc.net** or contact **Jane Maguire on 0141 551 4262** or **janemaguire@celticfc.co.uk**

CELTIC STORE DIRECTORY

GLASGOW STORES

The Celtic Superstore,
Celtic Park,
Glasgow
G40 3RE
Tel: 0141 551 4231

The Celtic Store,
215 Sauchiehall Street,
Glasgow
G2 3EX
Tel: 0141 353 1488

The Celtic Store,
154 Argyle Street,
Glasgow
G2 8BX
Tel: 0141 204 1588

The Celtic Store,
Terminal Building,
Glasgow Airport,
PA3 2SW
Tel: 0141 842 7846

www.celticsuperstore.co.uk

STORES IN THE REST OF SCOTLAND

The Celtic Store,
Unit 26,
The Thistle Centre,
Stirling
FK8 1EE
Tel: 01786 450615

The Celtic Store,
99 Sylvana Way,
Clyde Shopping Centre,
Clydebank
G81 2TL
Tel: 0141 941 1925

The Celtic Store,
24 West Mall,
The Plaza,
East Kilbride
G74 1LW
Tel: 01355 590538

The Celtic Store,
5 West Blackhall Street,
Greenock
PA15 1UA
Tel: 01475 888 140

The Celtic Store,
72 Main Street,
Coatbridge
ML5 3BQ
Tel: 01236 427399

The Celtic Store,
112 Seagate,
Dundee
DD1 2ET
Tel: 01382 223875

The Celtic Store,
36 Eastgate,
Inverness
IV2 3NA
Tel: 01463 713443

STORES IN IRELAND

The Celtic Store,
30-34 Ann Street,
Belfast
BT1 4EG
Tel: 02890 239111

The Celtic Store,
Unit 10,
1st Floor,
125 Upper Abbey Street,
Dublin 1
Tel: +3531 878 6856